Consciousness

Consciousness

William G. Lycan

A Bradford Book
The MIT Press
Cambridge, Massachusetts
London, England

This book was set in Palatino by Graphic Composition, Inc., and printed and bound by Halliday Lithograph in the United States of America.

Library of Congress Cataloging-in-Publication Data

Lycan, William G.
  Consciousness.

  "A Bradford book."
  Bibliography: p.
  Includes index.
  1. Consciousness.   I. Title.
  B105.C477L93   1987   126   87-4194
  ISBN 0-262-12124-7

This book is for my daughter Jane, with much love.

Contents

Preface

Some mental states have "feels" or qualitative phenomenal characters. And since the dawn of Behaviorism, some philosophers have doubted the ability of any physicalist account of the mental to accommodate this fact. There is something it is like, or feels like, to be in pain or to hear middle C as played by Dennis Brain or to have one's visual field suffused with vivid yellow; how could the introspectible qualitative features of such states as these possibly be explained, explicated, afforded, or even allowed by a theory that reduces persons and their states fo the motions of dull little atoms in the void? That is the main question that concerns me in this book. In answer to it I shall develop and defend the theory of mind that I call Homuncular Functionalism, arguing that the view is entirely adequate to the subjective phenomenal character of the mental and to all the facts of consciousness.

Incidentally, the terms "conscious" and "consciousness" have any number of different though related senses: A being is a conscious as opposed to a *non*conscious being if (unlike a stick or a stone) it has the *capacity* for thought, sensation, and feeling even if that capacity is never exercised, as in the case of an infant that dies soon after birth. A creature is conscious as opposed to *un*conscious if it is awake and having occurent mental states such as pains, perceivings, and episodic beliefs and desires. But (see chapter 6) there is a further, introspective or attentive sense in which even such episodic states of subjects can themselves be unconscious or, better, subconscious, "unfelt"—not to mention Freud's even more special sense. There is the dyadic consciousness *of* some physical or perhaps intentionally inexistent item. There is one's consciousness or awareness *that* such-and-such is the case. There is the vaunted *self*-consciousness or even "consciousness of self." And more. We shall see that all these notions are different, and that insofar as any of them poses problems for physicalism, the respective problems are very different problems and must be dealt with quite separately. Thus my title is a misnomer or at least a malnomer, and I admit that in choosing it I have just pandered to currently popular usage. What really concern me are the qualitative features or phenomenal characters of mental items, in a sense finally to be clarified in chapter 8.

This book is a very distant descendant of what was to have been a joint work by George Pappas and me, and has been cited in the literature under the title *Materialism*. Sometime during the 1970s, both Pappas and I lost interest in doing our original project—essentially a critical survey of materialist theories of the mind—and I began proselytizing for Homunctionalism in particular, with the results ensuing. I am grateful to Pappas for rich and rigorous discussion over the years. I am also indebted to generations of graduate students at the Ohio State University, the University of Sydney, and the University of North Carolina for their many critical and constructive contributions; to David Armstrong and Keith Campbell for numerous trenchant conversations about "qualia"; to Victoria University of Wellington for giving me the opportunity to present this material in the form of a course of lectures in 1986; and to David Rosenthal and Robert van Gulick for their more than generous comments on an earlier draft of this book. And as always, warm thanks to Harry and Betty Stanton for their patient encouragement and for their joint homuncular realization of the vigorous group organism called Bradford Books.

Acknowledgments

Chapter 3 partially reprints my articles "A New Lilliputian Argument against Machine Functionalism" (1979) and "The Moral of the New Lilliputian Argument" (1982), both reprinted by permission of *Philosophical Studies;* copyright © 1979/1982 by D. Reidel Publishing Company, reprinted by permission. Chapter 4 contains interfoliated chunks of my "Form, Function, and Feel" (1981), reprinted from the *Journal of Philosophy* by permission. Sections 1–4 of chapter 7 are lifted from "Phenomenal Objects: A Backhanded Defense," in J. Tomberlin (ed.), *Philosophical Perspectives,* Vol. 1. The appendix borrows about four pages from "Abortion and the Civil Rights of Machines," in N. Potter and M. Timmons (eds.), *Morality and Universality,* copyright © 1986 by D. Reidel Publishing Company, reprinted by permission.

Consciousness

Chapter 1

Consciousness and Nature

Philosophers and psychologists pondering the mind/body relation often speak of "*the* problem of consciousness"—as if there were some single, well-defined issue that bore that title. In earlier days, there was not considered to be *so much as* one such question, for Descartes had succeeded in promoting the idea that the mind is better known than the body and that the immediate objects of consciousness are diaphanously revealed to the conscious subject. To quote even an eminent twentieth-century physicist, Sir Arthur Eddington: "Mind is—but you know what mind is like, so why should I say more about its nature?" (1935, p. 271). Rather, it was the nature—indeed the very existence—of the allegedly public, physical world that was felt to be dubious or at least dubitable, from within one's private movie theater.[1]

This Cartesian first-person perspective dominated the philosophy of mind, as well as metaphysics and epistemology generally, from the seventeenth century through the first half of our own. But its grip began to loosen in the 1940s and 1950s, upon collision with the verificationism that had come to pervade both philosophy and psychology.

1. Dualism and Behaviorism

A logical positivist or other verificationist whose favored "observation language" featured sense-datum statements could remain comfortably ensconced within the first-person perspective and insist on stating verification-conditions in terms of private sensory events. But some of the positivists whose interests were primarily scientific and meta-scientific could not in good conscience confine their observation languages to sense-datum vocabulary, since (a) the *private-sensory* verification-condition for a sophisticated scientific hypothesis, or even for a fairly straightforward statement about a gross macroscopic object, would be far too complex ever to state explicitly, even if it is granted that some such determinate condition exists, and (b) as they are still, intersubjectivity and the repeatability of experiments were felt to be essential to the scientific enterprise, but are unavailable to the sense-datum theorist. Positivism therefore moved in the direction of an interpersonally shared observation language, featuring gross macroscopic data taken to be directly observable albeit public.[2] The public verification-conditions of mental ascriptions are obviously behavioral—hence methodological behaviorism in psychology and Analytical Behaviorism in philosophy.

Both behaviorisms were additionally fueled by an independently growing dissatisfaction with Cartesian Dualism considered as a theory of the mental. This dissatisfaction had two main sources: (i) Cartesian minds or egos were increasingly felt to be ontological excrescences, neither sanctioned by our ordinary talk about the mental (as was persuasively shown by Ryle's rhetorical *tour de force* in *The Concept of Mind*, 1949), nor needed for the explanation of any publicly shared commonsensical fact. Have we any more reason to believe in them than in ghosts, ectoplasm, or spookstuff of any other sort? (ii) The well-known problem of causal interaction, intensely troubling even to Descartes himself, was felt to be insoluble. Indeed, one might fairly characterize Dualism as being virtually an official announcement that the mind/body problem is forever insoluble: *O magnum mysterium!*—the mind unquestionably interacts causally with the body, but we could not in principle even begin to discover how.[3] These general discomforts were later to be supplemented by more specifically scientistic concerns. (iii) In interacting causally with their associated bodies' perceptual organs and muscles, Cartesian egos seemed to violate the conservation laws of physics, notably the law governing matter-energy. Once this was recognized, Dualism became a sharply testable hypothesis. Suppose we were to lift off the top of a person's skull, under local anesthetic, and examine the still normally functioning brain beneath. Suppose we were to see the electrical energy generated by the subject's surface receptors come up the afferent pathways only to disappear into thin air. Shifting over to the efferent side of the central nervous system, we further see energy coming in apparently out of nowhere—created *ex nihilo*, physically speaking—and activating motor responses eventuating in muscle contractions. After painstaking and very unsettling investigation, we conclude that matter-energy simply is not conserved inside human skulls, though everywhere else it is. This would be a dramatic empirical confirmation of Dualism. But it is also laughably unlikely to happen. I would not envy anyone the task of suggesting to our colleagues in the physics department that this sort of observational result is *even faintly* to be expected, on purely philosophical grounds or any other.[4] Rather, it is a sure bet that upon opening up our subject's skull and deploying our (science-fictionally subtle and delicate) microscopic instruments, we would find nicely closed causal chains taking constellations of receptor stimuli neatly, though in a fabulously complex tangle, through the central nervous system (CNS) and out the efferent pathways onto sets of motor impulses issuing directly in behavior, without even a hint of matter-energetic irregularity.[5]

(iv) Evolutionary theory impugns Dualism also, in reminding us that humans are *at least* animals, a biological species descended from hominids and from even earlier ape-like creatures by the usual dance of random variation and natural selection (cf. Churchland, 1984, pp. 20–21). The evolutionary process has proceeded in all other known species by increasingly complex configurations of molecules, grouping them into organs and then into organ systems including *brains* supporting psychologies however primitive. Our human psychologies are admittedly more advanced, and breathtakingly so, but they are undeniably continuous with those of lower animals (a human infant must grow to mature adulthood by slow degrees), and we have no biological or other scientific reason to suspect that Mother Nature (as subserved by population genetics) somewhere, somehow created immaterial Cartesian egos in addition to all her cells, organs, organ systems, and organisms.

Both behaviorisms, psychological and philosophical, overturned the first-person perspective and imposed an external or third-person way of addressing what remained of the mind.[6] This third-person perspective may originally have been as much an artifact of positivism as the first-person view was of Descartes' distinctive mode of meditating, but owing in part to considerations (iii) and (iv) above it survived the death of positivism, and noticeably so, in that Behaviorism's successor, as much a creature of scientific realism as Behaviorism was of positivism, staunchly preserved it. To explain all this, let me quickly and crudely review the several objections that eventually vanquished Behaviorism by showing it to be a gross overreaction to the repugnance of Dualism.

2. Disadvantages of Behaviorism

(A) Introspectivist or "First-Person" Objections

For the Behaviorists, mental "states" were counterfactual states, or better, counterfactual *relations* obtaining in a person between stimuli hypothetically received by that person's receptor surfaces and his or her responsive behavior, as in "If you were to ask Jones what he thought of motorcycles, he would say, 'They are dangerous,' and if you were to ask him if motorcycles were dangerous, he would say, 'Yes,' and if you were to offer him a ride on a motorcycle, he would decline." Behaviorists made no mention of inner goings-on in the person that are introspectible by the person but inaccessible to direct public observation; inner goings-on of this sort were just the sorts of things the Behaviorists were concerned to disown.[7] But many philosophers felt that that was simply to overlook the most crucial aspects of sensory states at least: the states' felt phenomenal characters, introspectible by their owners. The Behaviorists were simply denying (in the name of alleged scientific rigor) what is obvious to any normal person: that some mental states and events are *episodic inner* states of persons, states that may be only very loosely connected to particular behavior patterns if at all. Consider a situation in which you are lying in bed, calmly looking up at the yellow ceiling and contemplating its color. You are having a visual experience of yellow—a static, homogeneous yellow expanse. This visual state is a monadic inner state of you; it is not merely a counterfactual relation somehow hosted by you. If any counterfactual behavior pattern is associated with being in this state (such as a disposition to shout "YES!" if asked "Is your ceiling yellow?"), they are *grounded in* this state, i.e., it is this state *in virtue of which* the counterfactual relations consequently obtain.

Many people understood Behaviorism as being a doctrine that no one could seriously believe; they said that Behaviorists when on duty were pretending to be anesthetized. Unfortunately, just as some Behaviorists' manic hostility to Cartesianism made them overreact violently against any use of mental talk, some more recent philosophers' manic hostility to Behaviorism has made them overreact against materialism in any form.[8]

(B) Inverted Spectrum
Behaviorism as I understand it entails that if persons *A* and *B* are behaviorially indistinguishable (if they do not differ even in their behavioral dispositions), then they are mentally indistinguishable. But suppose that through neurologic birth defect a person sees colored objects abnormally: he sees green when we see red, blue when we see yellow, etc. (We could make this more precise and plausible by specifying some non-homomorphic one-one mapping of the colors onto themselves, though there are some serious technical difficulties involved in getting all the similarity- and other relational properties mapped (Harrison, 1973; Hardin, 1985).) If our victim has had his condition from birth, then barring futuristic neurophysiological research no one will ever detect it. He would have learned the color words in the same way we learned them. He would have learned to

call red things "red," for example, because he would think that the color he sees phenomenally (green) is called "red," even though it is not. He would behave toward stop signs, Carolina T-shirts, etc., just as we do. He would be behaviorally indistinguishable from us.

It follows given Behaviorism that the "inverted spectrum" sufferer is mentally indistinguishable from us; if he were really seeing green when we were seeing red, there would have to be some at least potential behavioral mark or symptom. The Behaviorist must maintain that inverted spectrum is conceptually or at least metaphysically *impossible*, and that is very implausible. It is unsettling at best to have what seems to be an entirely empirical issue legislated for us in advance.[9]

(C) "Absent Qualia"
We might fashion an anthropoid shape out of some light, pliable metal and cover it with plastic skin for the sake of verisimilitude, making it look just like a human being. Call it the Tinfoil Man. It is completely hollow except for some transceivers inside that pick up signaled instructions and trigger primitive peripheral motor units inside the tinfoil shell. The signalled instructions come, of course, from a console hidden elsewhere, operated by a team of zany electronic wizards, human puppeteers, who as a practical joke make the Tinfoil Man "behave" in ways appropriate to (what they and we can observe to be) events in its environment and to the "stimuli" that impinge on it. In virtue of the puppeteers' skillful handling, all the Behaviorist's counterfactuals are true of the Tinfoil Man. Thus, the Behaviorist is committed to ascribing all sorts of mental states to the Man, which is absurd, because "he" is a mere mock-up, largely empty inside. (If the presence of the transceivers bothers you, we can remove them and have the Man operated by external magnets that serve as puppet "strings." Or we could just use the example of a real puppet.) The Tinfoil Man lacks the complexity of structure that would be required to produce genuine mental states and genuinely self-motivated behavior in any organism. (The complexity of structure that does suffice to produce the Tinfoil Man's realistically complex behavior is in the puppeteers' own brains and in the console.) Thus is Behaviorism counterexampled.[10]

(D) The Belief-Desire-Perception Cycle
Either the Analytical Behaviorist or the ordinary Reductive Behaviorist (who makes no claims about linguistic meaning) understands "Dudley believes that motorcycles are dangerous" as being true just in case Dudley avoids motorcycles, refuses to ride on them, refrains

from stepping in front of them when they are moving, warns his friends against them, recommends them warmly to his enemies, etc.—or rather, just in case Dudley is disposed to do these things (*would* do them) under appropriate circumstances whether or not he ever actually has occasion to do them.

The trouble with letting the matter go at that is that Dudley will be disposed to behave in those ways only if he is also in a certain *frame of mind* (cf. Chisholm, 1957; Geach, 1957). For example, he will refuse to ride on his grandmother's motorcycle (or so we may imagine) only because (a) he *perceives* it to be a motorcycle and (b) he *desires* not to have an accident. (And also only because he believes that riding dangerous vehicles leads to accidents, but let it pass.) Of course, normal people would perceive that it was a motorcycle if it presented itself to them under felicitous perceptual conditions, and people typically do desire not to have accidents, but that does not mitigate the inadequacy of the proposed analysis, since nothing in our sample belief-ascription guarantees that Dudley is normal or typical. The Behaviorist will have to retrench again: "*If* Dudley were to perceive that something is a motorcycle and desires not to have an accident [*and* has no other overriding desires or beliefs, *and* . . . , *and* . . .], he refuses to ride on that thing, etc., etc."

But this new explicans is not solely about behavior; it contains unexplicated mental expressions. We must now give a further Behaviorist explication of these. Consider desire, as in "Dudley wants a beer." The Behaviorist would begin by casting this as something like "When there is a beer within walking distance, Dudley will act in such a way as to obtain it and drink it, etc." But as before, this is inaccurate. Dudley will try to get the beer only because he *believes* that it is a beer; if he thought it was a foamy, frosty, inviting cyanide preparation he would at least have second thoughts. So our explicans would have to be rewritten as something like "Whenever Dudley believes of a thing that it is a beer in his vicinity, he will act in such a way as to obtain it and drink it, etc." Again, we may be able to explicate "desire" in this way, but we have succeeded only in defining it in terms of other mental states, and (worse) if we take this explication together with our earlier analysis of "belief," vicious circularity results. It seems safe to predict that any proposed Behaviorist analysis of a mental ascription will meet this fate; at least, I have never seen an even faintly promising contender. If so, then the Behaviorist's overall explicative/reductive program will crash, even if one or more of the individual explications compromised in it is correct. In effect, each mental term will be contextually explicated in terms of the others (all very well, as we shall see later on), but the mind *tout court* will remain *sui generis* and autonomous; Behaviorism as a *reductive* thesis will fail.[11]

Each of our four types of objection points toward the *inner*. And Behaviorism's successor, the Identity Theory, proved dramatically immune to them all, as I shall now explain. But similar objections will return to plague present-day Functionalism, and in particular my own Homuncular Functionalism, as well.

3. *The Identity Theory and Functionalism*

According to the Identity Theory (as I shall use that label[12]), mental states were after all both episodic and inner—indeed far more *literally* inner than the Cartesian Dualist might legitimately allow. In defiance of the Behaviorists, it was insisted that there is an "intractable residue" (Place, 1956) of conscious mental states that bear only slack and indefinitely defeasible relations to overt behavior of any sort; perhaps the best examples of such states are those that we usually describe in terms of their qualitative phenomenal characters, or "raw feels," typically involving sensory experience or mental imagery. By way of illustrating their resistance to explication wholly in terms of dispositions to behave, the Identity Theorists joined the refractory Dualists in making complaints of the four types recounted above, particularly the introspective and inverted-spectrum objections. In particular, though approving of the Behaviorists' anti-Cartesian stand, the Identity Theorists suggested that the Behaviorists had mislocated the mental among the physical aspects of human beings. Mental states are undeniably inner after all; they are the states that *mediate* between stimulus and response and are *responsible* for the overt input-output functions so dear to the Behaviorist. To wit, they are states of the central nervous system, describable in neuroanatomical terms.

There is a double-aspect aspect here. Mental states are to be *initially characterized*, analytically or at least commonsensically, solely in terms of their mediating role, but they will be *found to be* states of the CNS. Thus "role-occupant" reduction: we already know that something or other is doing so-and-so, and then eventually we shall discover what that thing is.

For example, if we ask what a *pain* is, we initially characterize it in terms of its typical external causes and effects: it is the sort of inner state that results from damage and issues in withdrawal-and-favoring behavior; when we then open up an organism and look inside, we find what sort of state that is, e.g., a firing of c-fibers.[13]

This shift of location, from peripheral transactions to neurophysiological activity, was felt to be a great theoretical advance. But in the

1960s Hilary Putnam and others (Putnam, 1967; Fodor, 1968b; cf. Lycan, 1974b) exposed a presumptuous implication of the Identity thesis construed as a theory of mental *types* or kinds: that any conceivable being (mammal, mollusc, or Martian) would have to have a neurophysiology just like ours in order to have beliefs, to suffer pain, or what have you. By specifying the scientific natures of mental states as narrowly as Place and Smart seemed to intend (in terms of specific sorts of neural fibers in the brain), the Identity Theorist placed indefensibly strong constraints on the biology of any entity that was to be admitted as a possible subject of mental states or events, and so became a species chauvinist. It became clear that the Identity Theorists had overreacted to the Behaviorists' difficulties and become far *too* concerned with the specifics of humans' actual inner state-tokens. We may hold onto our anti-Cartesian claim that mental state- and event-*tokens* are identical with organic state- and event-tokens in their owners, but we would do better to individuate mental types more abstractly, in terms (let us say) of the functional roles their tokens play in mediating between stimuli and responses. Putnam proposed to identify mental state- and event-types with roles of this sort, rather than with whatever various physiological states or events happened to play these roles in various humans and nonhumans from occasion to occasion; thus, he moved back in the direction of Behaviorism in order to correct the Identity Theorists' overreaction.

Encouraged by the fruitfulness of comparing humans and other sentient organisms to computing machines, Putnam and others implemented their Functionalist idea in terms of machine programs that would detail the functional relations between possible "inputs," possible "outputs," and the various inner states of the organism that figure abstractly in the production of outputs from inputs; Putnam envisioned a theory of mind whose explications of individual mental state-types would take the form "To be in a mental state M is to realize or instantiate machine program P and be in functional state S relative to P." Let us call the view that some such set of explications is correct *Machine Functionalism.*

For reasons that I have developed elsewhere (Lycan, 1979a) and shall briefly revisit in chapter 3, I do not believe any version of Machine Functionalism can succeed. Rather, I shall defend an ontology of the mental that is functionalist in a more robust sense of the term 'function' than that employed by the Machine theorist. But first we must take up some questions of essentialism as it applies to mental entities.

Chapter 2
Functionalism and Essence

The Analytical Behaviorists made materialism a conceptual truth. But Place, Smart, and Armstrong insisted that their mind-brain identity hypothesis was *contingent* and entirely *a posteriori*. This feature of the Identity Theory promptly gave rise to what came to be called the "topic-neutrality problem" (TNP), first encountered in the form of "Black's objection" to Smart[1] and then formulated and addressed explicitly by Armstrong (1968b). Since Saul Kripke (1971, 1972) has shown that we must be much more careful about our uses of the allied but distinct notions of contingency, empiricalness, syntheticity, etc., we ought to look back at the TNP in light of Kripke's work. We shall find that materialism is still up to its neck in modal claims.

1. *Topic-Neutrality*

The problem was that, if an identity-statement such as "My pain at *t* = the firing of my c-fibers at *t*" is substantive and *nontrivial* (as it certainly is), then the two expressions flanking the identity sign must be associated with distinct characteristic sets of identifying properties, in terms of which we make separate and dissimilar identifying references to what is claimed to be in fact one and the same thing. We know the identifying properties that are associated with the term "the firing of my c-fibers at *t*"; the problem is to isolate those that are associated with "my pain at *t*." Smart (perhaps), Armstrong, and Lewis (1966) (see also Bradley, 1969) all seem to have agreed that in order to find those identifying properties we must find some *synonym* for the expression "my pain at *t*" that expresses the identifying properties more directly and explicitly. (And, of course, the synonym would have to be topic-neutral, for the reasons that are now familiar.)

The question really ought to be raised of whether a program of *translations* is necessary for any solution to the TNP (or, for that matter, to avoid "Black's objection"). In fact, more recent commentators have shown that Bradley and Smart were both wrong in assuming so, on two grounds. First, synonymy of state-ascriptions is really too strong a requirement for identity of states or properties. For there seems to be contingent or *a posteriori* identity of states as well. Thus, the state of having a temperature of 70°C is identical with the state of being made of molecules whose mean kinetic energy is such-and-such, but ascriptions of these states to a single object are not synonymous. The test for this alleged contingent identity of states is more subtle and certainly more troublesome to formulate precisely, but certainly coarser-grained.[2]

The second point is far more penetrating. It is that mental ascriptions may in fact *be* topic-neutral even if no translations can be provided for them that show this.[3] There may be in English no *existing synonym* for some mental ascription; it does not follow that the meaning of that ascription is not topic-neutral. In fact, so far as has been shown, we may hold that mental states are identified topic-neutrally even if we have no explicit list of topic-neutral properties in terms of which they *are* identified. The onus is on Smart's or Armstrong's opponent to argue that mental ascriptions are actually mentalistic.

My claim receives additional support from the following general methodological point: Take any modal claim to the effect that some statement is necessarily or logically true. I would say that the onus of proof of this claim is on its proponent; a theorist who wants to hold that something that is not *obviously* impossible *is* nonetheless impossible owes us a justification for thinking so. Now, entailment claims are positive modal claims of this kind. Therefore, anyone who holds that some sentence S_1 entails a second sentence S_2 must defend this if it is controversial; such a person does not get to say, "You can't have a counterexample, because I just know you can't."[4] And the claim that mental ascriptions are mentalistic rather than topic-neutral is an entailment claim, while the claim that they are topic-neutral is the denial of one. So the Identity Theorist may quite properly sit back and demand that his opponent *prove* that the Identity Theory is untenable in virtue of mental ascriptions' containing some mentalistic element. He need not shoulder the initiative and go off in search of a set of correct translations, or even of a precise set of topic-neutral identifying properties.[5]

2. Kripke's Argument against Token Identity

As all the world knows, Kripke has mounted a modal argument—specifically, an essentialist argument—against materialism, based on his distinction between rigid and nonrigid or flaccid designators, a rigid designator being one that denotes the same object at every possible world at which that object exists. I reconstruct Kripke's argument as follows.[6]

(N)   Every true identity-statement whose terms are rigid designators is necessarily true [or rather, true at every world at which the common referent exists].

This follows from the definition of rigidity.[7]

(R)   In the identity-statement "My pain at t = my c-fiber stimulation at t," both terms are rigid.

This is because each term characterizes its referent noncontingently; my pain at t is essentially a pain, and my c-fiber stimulation (cfs) at t is essentially a cfs. Further:

(D)   If a and b are "distinguishable" in the sense that we seem to be able to imagine one existing apart from the other, then it is possible that $a \neq b$, *unless* (i) "someone could be, *qualitatively* speaking, in the same epistemic situation" *vis-à-vis* a and b, and still "in such a situation a *qualitatively* analogous statement could be false," or [let us add] (ii) there exists some third alternative explanation of the distinguishability of a and b.

Kripke's model for (D-i) is the distinguishability of heat from molecular motion. Though heat is identical with molecular motion and necessarily so, the characteristic sensation-of-heat (the feeling produced in us by heat) is only contingently caused by molecular motion. Thus I could be in the same "epistemic situation" with respect to heat even if something other than molecular motion were producing my sensation-of-heat, and that is why heat *seems* separable from molecular motion even though it is not. Now:

(1)   My pain at t and my cfs at t are distinguishable.

Let us try to suppose that the model of heat and molecular motion applies.

(2)   If I can be, "qualitatively speaking, in the same epistemic situation" *vis-à-vis* my pain and my cfs and still "in such a situation a qualitatively analogous statement could be false," then either (a) my pain (= my cfs) could have occurred without constituting or producing my sensation-of-pain, or (b) my sensation-of-pain could have occurred without having been constituted or produced by my pain (= my cfs).

But a pain *just is* a sensation-of-pain and vice versa; unlike physical instances of heat, pains are themselves feelings, mental entities. Thus:

(3) Not-(2-a) and not-(2-b). "To be in the same epistemic situation that would obtain if one had a pain *is* to have a pain; to be in the same epistemic situation that would obtain in the absence of pain *is* not to have a pain. . . ." [Let us call these denials of (2-a) and (2-b) the "transparency theses."]

So:

(4) It is not true that I could be "qualitatively speaking, in the same epistemic situation" *vis-à-vis* my pain and my cfs and still "in such a situation a qualitatively analogous statement could be false"; (D-i) is refuted. [2,3]

Moreover:

(5) There does not exist any third alternative explanation of the distinguishability of my pain and my cfs; (D-ii) is to be rejected also. [Kripke says that the case of heat and molecular motion is "the only model [he] can think of" for the pain/cfs situation.]

Since (D-i) and (D-ii) fail for the case of pain/cfs:

(6) If my pain and my cfs are distinguishable, then it is possible that my pain ≠ my cfs. [1,4,5]
(7) If it is possible that my pain ≠ my cfs, then the identity-statement "My pain at t = my cfs at t" is not necessarily true.

So:

(8) The statement "My pain at t = my cfs at t" is not true; the Token Identity theory is false. [(1),(6),(7),(N),(R)]

I have criticized this argument in an earlier work (Lycan, 1974a), but I now think the objections I offered there were too crude, and I shall not repeat them here (at least in their original form). Rather, I shall make some new or at least considerably revised points against Kripke.

First, there is a problem about (2) and (3). I would maintain that Kripke equivocates on terms like "sensation of pain," and that the joint plausibility of (2) and (3) depends on this equivocation.

A "sensation of pain" could just be (redundantly) a *pain,* or it could be an additional cognitive/epistemic state—of awareness, say—directed upon a pain, as Kripke's talk of one's "epistemic situation" suggests. Suppose the former. Then we have no reason to accept (2), since (2-a) and (2-b) would be trivial contradictions in terms, while (2)'s antecedent is a substantive epistemological thesis. (Note too that (3) would be a mere tautology and so drop out of the argument.) Suppose, alternatively, that "sensation of pain" means a cognitive state of conscious awareness or the like. Then (2) is acceptable, but (3) turns into a strong incorrigibility doctrine to the effect that to be in pain at all *just is* to be consciously aware of pain and vice versa. Descartes would (naturally) have granted this, but materialists characteristically do not. Armstrong (1968b) in particular has antecedently argued against it in ways that do not presuppose the truth of materialism. So on this second interpretation Kripke relies on a tendentious, nearly question-begging assumption.

In fact, a more decisive charge of question-begging can be pressed. Note carefully that if we grant Kripke (3) on this strong interpretation, he *has no need of any of the rest of the argument—N, R, D,* or any of his "analytical tools"—for the falsity of the Identity Theory would fall right out *via* Leibniz's Law.[8]

The second interpretation and my Armstrongian response to it lead to a regress. A sensation-of-pain distinct from the pain itself would also have to be a brain state—a different one. (For example, one might follow Armstrong's (1968b) model and take conscious introspective awareness of the pain to be the output of a dedicated self-scanning device; I shall defend a version of this model in chapter 6.) So Kripke would just reiterate his argument with respect to it, and we are off and running.[9] But Armstrong has a plausible rejoinder: that the regress is in fact limited by the subject's actual psychological capacities, viz., by how many internal scanners the subject has actually got (cf. pp. 14–15 of Armstrong, 1981); a creature who runs out of scanners runs out of iterated awarenesses. There is a temptation to think that the awarenesses simply collapse into each other; a similar suggestion in epistemology leads to the nefarious "KK" thesis (that knowing entails knowing that one knows). But just as in the case of the "KK" thesis, the seeming collapse is easily explained: it occurs simply because we do not make such level distinctions very well in introspection.[10]

I turn to a problem about rigidity. There is a temptation (often indulged by contributors to the discussion of Kripke's argument) to think that the rigid/flaccid distinction divides the class of singular terms themselves, as expression-types. But this is an error. Expression-types are not *per se* rigid or flaccid; it is particular *uses* of expressions (particular tokens) that are rigid or flaccid. There is considerable variation from speaker to speaker and from utterance-occasion to utterance-occasion, especially in the context of philosophy of mind. To avoid the danger of ending up bickering over statistical frequencies of rigid versus flaccid uses, let us just say that sentences with singular terms in them may be *ambiguous* as between rigid and flaccid interpretations.

The complaint I wish to make about Kripke's *R* is obvious to any functionalist or other topic-neutralist regarding mental entities: that the relationalist's identity-statement is not intended rigidly, since the relationalist (Armstrong, Lewis, or Putnam) offers it as the outcome of a role-occupant reduction. In the relationalist's mouth, "My pain at t" is (normally) intended to designate whatever (presently unknown) physical state of a subject is doing φ, etc. Thus, his "identity-statement" is not a "genuine" one and Kripke's *N* does not apply to it; the argument is invalid.

Of course, "My pain at t" can be used rigidly—we can stick in an explicit stiffener, as in "*This very* pain that I have at t" or "My *actual* pain at t" or "The pain I have at t in the actual world." Then our identity-statement is a genuine one again (assuming "my cfs at t" is also rigid). But now the imaginabilities go haywire. It is by no means obvious that on this interpretation the identity-statement is not (if true) necessarily true, just as "Heat = molecular motion" is necessary if true on its standard rigid interpretation. It does not help to note (as Kripke does) that my cfs can occur without my being in pain, because it is possible, for all Kripke has *argued,* that the very state of me that in this world does φ (we might say, that "pains" for me here) also could occur, in another world, without my being in pain. Armstrong certainly would insist that the state that is in fact my pain *need* not have been a pain. And just as when I find out that *this* table is made of cellulose molecules I lose my ability to imagine a qualitatively similar table's being made of something else, when I find out that *this* pain is made of cfs I lose my ability to imagine *this* pain's being made of something else, though I keep my ability to imagine a qualitatively similar pain's being made of something else.[11] (The present point underscores the difficulty of saying what one is actually imagining when one seems to be imagining a state of affairs described in such-and-such a way.)

Kripke acknowledges the availability of this sort of move in "Naming and Necessity," but he asks, how could my *pain* have failed to be a *pain?* Can we say of a pain that it, that very pain, might have been something else?? This he proclaims "self-evidently absurd." (In my previous paper, 1974a, I replied that it cannot very well be *self-evidently* absurd, since it is precisely what a number of very intelligent people—even some fellow inhabitants of 1879 Hall—think; Kripke opined in response that the latter consideration does not suffice to rule out the self-evidence of an absurdity.)

Put back in terms of our rigid/flaccid ambiguity, Kripke's claim amounts to saying that "My pain at *t*" just *does not admit* any flaccid reading. The phrase simply picks out the pain in terms of a property that the pain has in all possible worlds, viz., being a pain or being painful, which Kripke identifies with the pain's "immediate phenomenological quality." There is, Kripke insists, nothing *roley* or *officey* about this at all.

Another impasse. But it is worth repeating my point, made more elaborately in Lycan (1974a), that imaginability follows science rather than the other way around. So I just have done.[12]

3. Dialectic and Diagnosis

Charges of question-begging are delicate and hard to adjudicate, so let me say another word about how I understand the two such charges I have made against Kripke. In each case, the point is simply that even if Kripke is right and Armstrong et al. are wrong, *this* argument of Kripke's does not show that, because it baldly assumes the falsity of two theses that Armstrong and others have already and independently defended. Our question as materialists (or presumptive materialists) entertaining "qualia"-based objections is, are there any antimaterialist arguments that work? We have looked at this argument of Kripke's, and it does not work. Perhaps some variation on it might work. I sincerely invite the reader to try to devise one; but there is no reason to reject materialism in the meantime.

I suggest that once the "analytical tools" have dropped out in the way they do, Kripke is revealed as being substantially (so to speak) a Cartesian. Let me expand that remark, since Kripke does not plump for immaterial substance in so many words, and indeed denies allegiance to Dualism (1972, Footnote 77). First, notice that if his argument works against cfss it works *mutatis mutandis* against any physical item—thus he is committed to the nonphysicalness of pains. What is additionally Cartesian about (2) and (v), apart from the fact of their entailing mind-brain distinctions in virtue of Leibniz's Law, is that they presuppose that the essence of the mental is its transparency to its subject. For pains, on this view, *esse est* appearing directly and diaphanously to their owners. One understands the word "pain" only by having felt pain. (Kripke once complained to me that one could read and understand Armstrong's *analysans* for pain and still not know what pain is. This ties neatly in with Nagel's argument, which we shall examine in chapter 7.) Of course, this is a key part of the Cartesian picture that the materialist is concerned precisely to reject.

What is Cartesian (and Russellian) about Kripke's insistence on *R* is a traditional connection between rigidity and ostension. The paradigm of a rigid designator is a "Millian" name or indexical, one that serves (semantically speaking) *just* to designate its referent and not to characterize that referent in any way. Rigid designators are very like logically proper names.[13] Such names are taught by *ostension* or by the offering of descriptive backings that "fix" their referents but not their senses. (Russell thought they could be taught only by ostension; that assumption was exploded by Kripke himself.) Now, if you have a pain, or a feeling you call "pain," I cannot learn its names by ostension because I cannot be directly acquainted with it (as was observed incessantly in the heyday of the Problem of Other Minds). I have to learn it by its descriptive backing, which would probably look just like an Armstrongian *analysans*. But on Kripke's view, unlike Armstrong's, that backing does not serve as an *analysans* because it does not fix sense; it does not tell me what the word "pain" *means,* but is only a contingent recipe for finding "pain"'s referent in the actual world. Thus, only you can know what "pain" means, by ostension. And that ostension is *private* ostension. Thus, Kripke will have to answer the very compelling arguments against this advanced by Dewey, Wittgenstein, Sellars, et al.[14] Besides, he has bought into or perhaps simply started from the very Movie-Theater Model of the mind that every materialist since Ryle has been concerned to trash.

4. A Final Criticism of Kripke and a First Encounter with the Banana Peel

Kripke's argument depends on the claim that pains' raw qualitative characters are essential to them. But remember a crucial point: The materialist denies that "pains" are *objects,* simply rejecting all phenomenal individuals such as sense-data. What the materialist identifies with brain items are rather mental states and events, in this case *the having of a pain* (better: the-having-of-a-pain, or *hurting*). If Kripke's essentialist thesis is to engage the materialist, then, it must be aimed at such pain-events rather than at "pains" construed as phenomenal individuals. But once this is made clear, the intuitive plausibility of Kripke's thesis evaporates. For *events do not have individual essences,* or at least we have no dependable *de re* modal intuitions regarding events.

Consider an example. You are sitting casually in an empty classroom, reading a book. Suddenly I burst in the door, holding a basketball, and proceed to bounce the basketball, very hard, on the floor. Then I leave. This episode was an event. What are its essential properties?—that is, what are the properties in virtue of which it was the event it was rather than a numerically different event? That I was its protagonist? That a basketball was used rather than a soccer ball? That the ball was bounced twice rather than three times, once, or not at all? That the episode took place in this classroom rather than the one next door? That it took place when it did instead of ten minutes earlier? None of these suggestions seems at all convincing, and I would maintain that events as such simply *do not have* individual essences unless their essences are very rarefied and elusive haecceities. If this is correct, then Kripke's claim that the phenomenal characters of pain-events (i.e., of episodes of hurting) are essential to those events is groundless or at least not in the least obvious—not nearly so obvious as it would have to be for Kripke's argument to succeed (dialectically speaking).

Kripke beguiles us into tacitly thinking of pains as individuals, as sense-data. That is the only reason anyone might be tempted to share his essentialist intuition or, I would say, any other essentialist intuition about pains. Once we decisively reject mental objects, Kripke's argument entirely loses its force even if we were to grant the points to which I have already objected.

There is an important general observation to be made here. Kripke is not alone in slipping tacitly from talk of mental states and events to what amounts to talk of phenomenal individuals. Other critics of materialism do this as well, *even critics who are ostensibly well aware* that contemporary materialists eliminate mental individuals and reduce only states and events. We shall see any number of cases of this. Indeed, the phenomenon is so prevalent and (until now) so widely unnoticed that I think it deserves a special name; I shall call it "the Banana Peel," since antimaterialists typically and question-beggingly slip on it into the Movie Theater Model of the mind.[15]

The pejorative adverb "question-beggingly" may be balked at. Suppose a critic of materialism maintains that *there are* phenomenal individuals such as pains and other sense-data, and that the typical materialist is just being perverse in refusing without argument to countenance them. That is, an antimaterialist may come out of the closet and insist, à la Jackson (1977), that far from slipping on the Banana Peel he is stoutly reminding us of the existence of phenomenal individuals and their *essential* properties. Then I would say, we are playing a very different game. For such an antimaterialist is hardly making an *argument* against materialism, and certainly no such sophisticated modal argument as Kripke's; rather, he has already abandoned physicalism of any sort. If there (really) are phenomenal individuals such as sense-data, then materialism is false *right there;* no further reasoning is needed. On the other hand, one is stuck with making a case for phenomenal individuals and with turning aside all of the powerful objections to sense-datum theories. I shall postpone consideration of that issue until chapter 8.

5. Topic-Neutrality and Essence

Even if the TNP as traditionally conceived is no real problem at all, since we are under no obligation to meet the demand that gives rise to the "problem" in the first place, it may be considered embarrassing that I use the referring term "my pain at *t*" freely without being able to produce a set of identifying properties (i.e., without being able to answer the question, "Your pain at *t?* What thing is that?"). It would still be nice to have a list of these identifying properties that we could produce on demand. For this reason, the attempts by Smart, Armstrong, and Lewis to provide topic-neutral translations are not entirely valueless. Besides, these attempts have also illuminated the methodological and epistemic routes by which their authors have arrived at the Identity Theory; in Armstrong (1968b) and Lewis (1966, 1972), the translations have figured as premises in deductive arguments for it. So perhaps we should continue to seek topic-neutral translations after all. At this point, though, I think it will be fruitful to reconstrue the TNP in a way suggested by Kripke's work.

Why did Place, Smart, and Armstrong fall all over themselves insisting that their posited identity was a "contingent" one? Historically, they maintained this because the identity was something that (if true) obviously would have to be *discovered* to hold by empirical scientists (cf. lightning and electrical discharge, the Morning Star and the Evening Star, etc.). And it seemed to every pre-Kripkean that anything whose discovery required empirical work was something that could have been otherwise and hence was contingent. But this move was blocked by Kripke, who pointed out that truths can be empirical and still necessary; genuine identities are examples of this. Therefore it is in fact *open* to the Identity Theorist to claim that a sentence such as "My pain at *t* = the firing of my c-fibers at *t*" is a necessary truth after all, albeit an empirical one; scientific identities in general are necessary though empirical identities.

But if "My pain at *t* = the firing of my c-fibers at *t*" is necessary, is it not therefore trivial? Given the fact that that identity-statement is *not* trivial but substantive, perhaps we ought not to take the line I have just suggested? But that depends on what we mean by "trivial."

Following Kripke, I maintain that what people really have (or should have) in mind when they insist that the Identity Theorist's identities are nontrivial is only that the identities are surprising, startling, something one may well not have known before. In short, the identities' nontriviality is *epistemic*. So we can after all maintain both that the identities are necessary and that they are substantive in the relevant (= the epistemic) sense.

In Kripke's terminology, if we provide a "backing of descriptions" for a referring term (alternatively, if we associate a set of identifying properties with that term) and if we do this successfully intending to "fix" the term's *sense*, then the term as used by us designates nonrigidly, or flaccidly. In particular, if a referring term is being used in an identity-statement and has had its sense fixed in that context by some backing of identifying descriptions, then that term is being used nonrigidly and the "identity"-statement is in a Russellian sense not a *genuine* identity-statement at all; I would explicate this sense by saying that the "identity"-statement is logically equivalent to a much simpler sentence that is predicative (thus the *identity* part is redundant and superfluous). More importantly, the predicative sentence to which our "identity"-statement is equivalent will be contingent, not necessary. Suppose that prior to using the sentence "The President of the United States is Ronald Reagan" in some context, I have fixed the *sense* of "The President of the United States" by saying "The President of the United States is the person who was last elected by such-and-such a process to the highest executive office in America." Then the sentence "The President of the United States is Ronald Reagan" is (on Russellian grounds) equivalent to "Ronald Reagan was last elected by such-and-such a process to the highest executive office in America," which is a contingent subject-predicate sentence.

Therefore: If the Identity Theorist wants to accept my suggestion and claim that his identities are necessary rather than contingent, and if he also wants to continue to seek a backing of descriptions or set of identifying properties to associate with mental terms such as "my pain at t," then he must make sure that he does not intend his backing of descriptions to fix the sense of "my pain at t." In pre-Kripkean times this would have been considered impossible, since it was widely thought (particularly by Wittgensteinians) that to provide a backing of descriptions for a term *had* to fix the sense of that term. But what Kripke showed was that sometimes when we provide a backing of descriptions for a term we do *not* fix the sense of the term, but merely "fix its reference." And so the Identity Theorist who intends his identities to be necessary has the option of finding some identifying topic-neutral "translations" that fix only the reference, and not the sense, of mental terms. (Thus, the "translations" would not be regarded as meaning- or sense-preserving, but only as helpful reference-fixing heuristics.)

Seeing that the Identity Theorist now has this option, we may ask any of its proponents which choice he would make in the matter. I shall not slog back through our Identity Theorists' Hall of Fame and calculate each counterfactual decision,[16] but I shall note some crucial consequences that such a choice would have for the Identity Theorists' abilities to meet the objections we have raised.

It is reasonable to continue to take Smart (of 1959) as an unabashed Type-Type theorist:[17] Mental states' similarities to what is going on in their owners when . . . is *not* essential to them, but is only alluded to as a way of telling us what states, neurophysiological states, Smart is talking about. As we have seen, a Type-Identity Theory of this kind avoids all our objections to Behaviorism, but it is not empirically plausible in the least, being crassly chauvinist.

It is equally reasonable *not* to take Armstrong as a Type-Type theorist. Certainly he never asserts the Identity Theory, and if confronted with its chauvinist implications, would probably join Lewis and the other liberals. He is also quite serious about his "causal analyses" *as analyses,* and so I shall understand those analyses as sense-fixing and interpret Armstrong as claiming that the *essential* (not merely the identifying) properties of mental entities are their characteristic causal roles, or rather, that *to be* a mental entity (of such-and-such a type) is to play causal role so-and-so; thus he is an out-and-out relationalist.[18]

On this interpretation, Armstrong is able to renounce chauvinism. On the other hand, as a relationalist, he thereby exposes himself to the *sorts* of dangers that plagued Behaviorism—in particular, to the objections based on the Belief-Desire-Perception cycle, on inverted spectrum, and on "absent qualia." Until one looks at his view in meticulous detail, it is a bit hard to determine whether such objections really pose a problem for him. On the one hand, his apparent relationalism suggests that they do; but he called himself an Identity Theorist, after all, and the Identity Theory was devised precisely to be immune to objections of that kind. In the light of Kripke's work, we now see what the confusion was: we had not been told Armstrong's view on the *essence* of the mental. He must *choose between* metaphysical relationalism and the Type-Identity Theory construed as being a theory of the *nature* of what it is to be mental.

Once he chooses the former, as I have just suggested he would, he is subject to at least two of the standard objections: He will be able to accommodate inverted spectrum only if he introduces enough complexity into his system of causal roles to allow him to depict one and the same overt behavior-pattern as being produced by two hetero-morphic systems of causal dispositions; and he will have to resist "absent qualia" arguments. Lewis, whose view differs from Arm-strong's only in the exact content of its corresponding "postulate," is in precisely the same position.[19]

The upshot of all this is that the would-be Identity Theorist has (and must make) a few choices that no one noticed prior to 1971; and the choices have rather serious repercussions. So it seems Kripke's work, and in particular his "analytical tools," do not *simply* "drop out" after all.[20]

Chapter 3
Stalking the Tinfoil Man

As I have observed, any type-identification of mental entities with physical items entails modal claims. In particular, if what it is to be in a mental state of type M *simply is* to be in such-and-such a state of type T, then it is metaphysically necessary that an organism is in M iff that organism is in T. If Behaviorism is correct, then necessarily an organism is in pain iff it has the relevant behavioral dispositions. If the Identity Theory is correct, then necessarily an organism is in pain iff its c-fibers are firing; and so on.

Being modal generalizations, consequences of the foregoing sort are open to imaginative counterexample. If there should be seen to be a metaphysically possible creature that is in pain but has not the relevant behavioral dispositions or vice versa, then Behaviorism is false, and if there should be seen to be a metaphysically possible creature that is in pain but has no c-fibers firing or vice versa, then the Identity Theory is false. And we have noted in chapter 1 that there are indeed creatures of each type. The Tinfoil Man is an example of the first; the mollusk or Martian is an example of the second. In each case, we can not only suppose without self-contradiction that the requisite creature exists, but say in at least a bit of detail how the creature works and why it would or would not have mental states.

Some philosophers have claimed that Functionalism is open to counterexample in just the same sort of style. Functionalism entails that necessarily, any creature that feels pain must be in such-and-such a type of functional state and vice versa, but the philosophers in question have alleged the metaphysical possibility of one or another creature that has pain but not the requisite functional organization, or (more commonly) that is in the right functional state but feels no pain. Ned Block's (1978) "homunculi-head" cases are a notorious example.

As we have seen, standard Functionalist theories thus imply that having a set of purely relational properties suffices to make some inner state of a person a mental state. Block in effect deplores this consequence. I shall argue that despite the initial intuitive appeal of his attempt, it fails. But I shall go on to offer a somewhat similar counterexampling argument that I believe does inflict serious damage on Machine Functionalism (hereafter "MF").

1. Block's Examples

Block contends that no functional, causal, or otherwise purely relational theory of the nature of mental states can account for those states' purely qualitative, introspectible surface features, their "qualia" or immediate phenomenal feels. More specifically, Block may be understood as arguing that no specification of an organism's functional organization, however complex, could suffice to determine the respective qualitative characters of that organism's pains, visual sensations, and what have you. Two organisms might well share the same functional organization and all the same machine programs and still have their visual color spectra *inverted* relative to each other; in fact,

> For all we know, it may be nomologically possible for two psychological states to be functionally identical (that is, to be identically connected with inputs, outputs, and successor states), even if only one of the states has a qualitative content. In this case, functionalist theories would require us to say that an organism might be in pain even though it is feeling *nothing at all*, and this consequence seems totally unacceptable. (P. 173)

Block goes on to develop this attack on Functionalism at length, maintaining that it is quite possible, or seems quite possible, for something to share the functional organization of a sentient being and yet not be (phenomenally) conscious, in the sense of having qualia, at all—there might not be "anything it is like to be" that thing, as Nagel (1974) puts it, while there is certainly something it is like to be that thing's sentient functional twin.

It is fairly clear that as it stands this "absent qualia" argument begs the question. First, let us not forget that the machine programs we humans instantiate are incredibly complex, and that any other object or organism that instantiated them would have a comparably complex physical structure and behavioral repertoire. Is it really possible to imagine something's sharing *my entire* many-levelled functional organization and still not being conscious in the way that I am? Well, perhaps it is; questions of this kind are notoriously difficult to answer definitively. But, second, even if we can imagine Block's "absent qualia" situation, our ability to do this does not refute MF, for to imagine that situation is simply to imagine MF's being false. Since MF is a scientific or quasi-scientific or at any rate *a posteriori* theory of mind, our ability to imagine its falsity is unsurprising, and has no bearing on the reasonableness of believing that MF is in fact true.

Quite aware that he has so far succeeded at best in promulgating an impasse between attractive theory and imaginative intuition, Block gives two more detailed examples to back up his claim. The first of these is a hypothetical case involving

> a body externally like a human body, say yours, but internally quite different. The neurons from sensory organs are connected to a bank of lights in a hollow cavity in the head. A set of buttons connect to the motor output neurons. Inside the cavity resides a group of little men. Each has a very simple task: to implement a 'square' of a reasonably adequate machine table [program] which describes you. On one wall is a bulletin board on which is posted a card from a deck in which each bears a symbol which designates one of the states specified in the machine table. . . . Each little man has the task corresponding to a single quadruple [= square of a Turing Machine table]. Through the efforts of the little men, the system described realizes the same (reasonably adequate) machine table as you do and is thus functionally equivalent to you. (P. 278)

To make the case slightly more personal, suppose that the brain matter were actually to be scooped out of your own head and that the job of realizing your present program were instantaneously to be taken over by a waiting corps of homunculi.

In Block's second example,

> We convert the government of China to functionalism, and we convince them that it would enormously enhance their international prestige if they realized a human mind for an hour. We provide each of the billion people in China (I chose China because it has a billion inhabitants) with a specially designed two-way radio which connects them in the appropriate way to other persons, and to the artificial body mentioned in the previous example. We replace the little men with a radio transmitter and receiver connected to the input and output neurons. Instead of a bulletin board, we arrange to have letters displayed on a series of satellites placed so that they can be seen all over China. Surely such a system is not physically impossible. It could be functionally equivalent to you for a short time, say an hour. (P. 279)

Each of Block's two cases is intended to illustrate the same simple point: It is absurd, he thinks, to suppose that the homunculi-headed system of the first example is conscious, has qualia, or has inner states that have qualitative character; there is nothing it is like to be that system, since the system consists only of a dutiful corps of none-too-bright little men passing pieces of cardboard from hand to hand. MF taken together with the fact that I am conscious and the stipulation that the homunculi are realizing my program entails that the homunculi-headed system is conscious, and therefore MF is false. Similarly, Block believes it would be silly to suppose that the population of China, taken as an aggregate, sports a conscious mental life for an hour just in virtue of its having succeeded by breathtaking organizational effort in realizing some human's program throughout that time. (Notice that it is not even necessary for Block's point that Chinese workers be connected via radio transceivers to a human or humanoid body. We could simply draw an artificial boundary around a certain large geographical area in the Chinese mainland, arbitrarily specify certain official entrance and exit gates at that boundary, and correlate designated sorts of traffic through those gates with the inputs and outputs tabulated in the human twin's program.) The moral is that a version of MF based even on the most elaborate and sophisticated *kind* of machine program is still too liberal or tolerant a view, in that it would award consciousness and qualia to organisms that very plainly do not have them.

Graphic though they are, Block's two examples cannot be considered conclusive,[1] since philosophers who have offered what they believe are good reasons in favor of accepting MF may well be inclined to swallow the consequence that a homunculi-head or the population of China would be conscious and have qualia under such bizarre circumstances. Again, the MFist might point out, it is easy to underestimate the complexity of a human being's program. For example, one may be misled by thinking that all the Mad Scientist who hires the homunculi has to do is to get them to realize one rather complex but manageable Turing Machine; in fact, the homunculi would have to realize fabulously many distinct machine programs simultaneously, right down to the very complicated subroutines that underlie even so (phenomenologically) simple a conscious state as sharp pain.[2] Perhaps it does seem that if someone were to scoop out my head and replace my brain matter with a corps of homunculi who busied themselves with index cards realizing my program, I would cease to have qualia—for how could an actual *quale* be produced by or in a mere aggregate of dull little men shuffling index cards about?—and so on. But as Block himself seems to hint (p. 293), a parallel point could be urged against brain matter itself: "Each *neuron* is a dull, simple little device that does nothing but convey electrical charge from one spot to another; just stuffing an empty head with *neurons* wouldn't produce *qualia—immediate phenomenal feels!*" But of course it does produce them, even if we cannot imagine how that happens. (I shall have more to say on this point in chapter 5.)

Block defends his cases against this second insinuation of question-begging as well. I believe the core of his attempt to back up his conservative intuitions about homunculi-heads is to be found in these remarks:

> Now there is good reason for supposing that [a homunculi-head system] has some mental states. Propositional attitudes are an example. Perhaps psychological theory will identify remembering that *P* with having 'stored' a sentence-like object which expresses the proposition that *P*. . . . Then if one of the little men has put a certain sentence-like object in 'storage', we may have reason for regarding the system as remembering that *P*. But . . . there is no such theoretical reason for regarding the system as having qualia. (P. 306)

I am not sure what reasons Block intends to pick out as being "such theoretical" reasons. Possibly he means reasons based on the knowledge (a) of what sort of activity psychological theory characterizes "having a quale" as really being, (b) of what the little men are actually doing with their index cards in order to make the homunculi-head behave as if he is having a quale, and (c) that the two coincide. But whether or not there are reasons of "this" sort depends entirely on what sort of activity a developed psychology *will* characterize "having a quale" as really being. And the MFist is, *inter alia*, predicting that psychology will in fact characterize "having a quale" in some machine-functional terms or other. So, if I have interpreted the quoted passage correctly, Block has still not established his point.[3]

In fact, there is one plausible line of argument to suggest that the epistemic burden is on Block rather than on the MFist (though as an epistemic point it might be taken to encourage metaphysical ultraliberalism): On the face of things, a being's engaging in, say, pain-behavior in appropriate circumstances is excellent (though certainly defeasible) evidence that that being is in pain.[4] In the presence of such behavior, a skeptic would have to come up with substantial defeating evidence in order to overrule the presumption of genuine pain; and similarly for other qualitative states. Now, by hypothesis, our homunculi-head engages in quite subtle "having-a-quale"-behavior (since it realizes the program of a fully acculturated human being). Accordingly, it seems, we have excellent evidence for concluding that the homunculi-head is having a quale, decisive in the absence of a fairly strong counterargument or body of counterevidence. Block clearly believes that the fact of the behavior's being *intentionally pro-duced* by the corps of unskilled but independently motivated homun-culi, and perhaps some other facts of that sort (cf. p. 32), should make us regard the "having-a-quale"-behavior as misleading evidence. I admit that the cynicism of the homunculi's coordinated performance puts me off. But does our intuitive disquiet over this have enough evidential status to warrant our suspending our usual tests for whether some being has qualia, or rather, our regarding these tests, though they are satisfied, as being overruled or defeated in this case? It is certainly not obvious that it does.

I conclude that Block has not succeeded in breaking what is at best a stalemate with the MFist. But his homunculi-head cases suggest further, new objections to MF, at least one of which seems to me quite telling (I excerpt it from Lycan, 1979a).

2. *The New Lilliputian Argument (and Its Correct Understanding)*

Consider an organism *O* that realizes some sentient-creature-type program, and that does so in virtue of containing (or being made of) a corps of homunculi who shuffle index cards about. And consider just one of these billions of homunculi, *h*, who (having a rich mental life of his own) is consciously thinking, as he shuffles, that it is very dark in his vicinity (inside the giant skull) and that index cards ought to be painted phosphorescently so that the workers can see them better. Now we may begin the argument:

(1)   To think consciously that index cards ought to be painted phosphorescently is to realize a certain functional state S_p relative to a program *P*. (MFist's claim)

Let us use the Turing Machine model for simplicity; it seems clear that the argument will generalize to any version of MF. So S_p is one among the set of functional or logical states S_i mentioned by the rel-evant Turing Machine program realized by *h*. That program also tab-ulates inputs s_i and outputs o_i. Therefore,

(2)   *h* realizes S_p. (1, our hypothesis)

Now, what is it for an organism to *realize* a particular Turing Ma-chine program? According to standard usage, it is just for there to be some one-one mapping that correlates a set of discrete (possible) physical inputs, physical states, and physical outputs of the organism with the abstract input-letters, logical-state symbols, and output-letters (respectively) appearing in the machine program, in such a way that for any instruction $I(S_i, s_i)$ of the program, the organism goes into the physical correlate of the appropriate value (S_k, s_i) of $I(S_i, s_i)$ whenever the organism is in the physical correlate of S_i and receives the physical correlate of s_i as input. An organism can be *shown* to realize a program P, then, whenever a correlation of this kind can be found holding between the organism and P.

Now let us *construct* a machine program M that is realized (in this sense) by our friend h's containing organism O. M will tabulate inputs a_i, outputs b_i, and functional or logical states M_k; and I shall stipulate (since I am constructing M *ad hoc*) that the following relation will hold between O and M:

> (Def)   For any i, O receives input a_i iff O's 'h' component (viz., h) receives whatever physical stimulus we would normally identify as its characteristic functional input s_i. For any j, O emits output b_j iff h emits its characteristic output o_j. And for any k, O is in state M_k iff h is in its characteristic functional state S_k.

Now that our machine program M has been constructed in this way, we may note that the relation defined by (Def) constitutes a correlation of the sort described above; so O realizes our defined machine program M. Of course, O's "realizing" M is trivially parasitic on the functional doings of O's component h. But the results are surprising:

(3) M is a relabeling or notational variant of h's Turing Machine program containing S_p. [Obvious, from (Def)]

(4) $M_p = S_p$. (3)

(5) O realizes M_p iff h realizes S_p. (Def)

(6) O realizes M_p. (2,5)

(7) O realizes S_p. (4,6)

(8) O is thinking consciously that index cards ought to be painted phosphorescently. (1,7)

A parallel argument could be constructed for any other mental state occurring in any of O's component homunculi. Therefore, MF entails that a homunculi-head or other group person such as O would be *himself having* any mental state occurring in any of his constitutive horde of homunculi. Were I to turn out to be a homunculi-head, I would (or could) have thousands of explicitly contradictory beliefs (and there would be indexical problems too); further, despite my overwhelming inclination to deny it, I would have conscious awareness of each of my homunculi's conscious mental lives. But this seems outrageous and probably incoherent. If so, then it seems MF is far too liberal, and false.

This argument has a faint air of hokum (and in its previous publication has been curiously misunderstood by a number of otherwise astute critics, despite being truth-functionally valid). But it has no *obvious* flaw. One might protest the arbitrariness of my choice of the interpretive correlation recorded in (Def); but one would then bear the onus of proposing *and motivating* a suitable restriction on the kinds of correlation in virtue of which some physical structure may be said to "realize" a particular abstract machine program. This will be my own strategy in the chapters to come, but it will be tricky. Note that the notion of "realization" that I defined above *has been the going notion*, appealed to (so far as I can see) by every MFist in the literature. The present suggested response to my argument would prevent the MFist's being able to make do with this nice, crisp formal notion of realization. But much of MF's appeal has derived from this crispness, and any of the various repairs that might be made will very likely introduce obscurities and vagueness.[5]

Now, one might balk even earlier on, and contend that h is not really a *component* of O in any interesting or relevant sense; but this would be a hard position to defend, since (we may suppose) h performs an identifiable job for O and plays a significant (if small) role in maintaining O's mental activity. One might also complain that I have made an unfair choice of a mental state to use in my example; but on what grounds? Finally, one might relinquish the letter of the MFist's schema, "To be in mental state M is to realize or instantiate machine program P and be in functional state S relative to P," refining it in some further way that is hard to extrapolate from present functionalist views.

As I have said, I shall be pursuing the first of the strategies just mentioned: restricting our notion of "realization" or instantiation of a program. But first it is necessary to comment further on the foregoing New Lilliputian Argument (NLA) in order to forestall some misunderstandings that (I have found) often greet it.

As I have used the term, "Machine Functionalism" is the view that a correct metaphysical explication of a particular mental state (-type) would take the form "To be in mental state M is to realize or instantiate machine program P and to be in functional state S relative to P," where a physical organism or system O *realizes* or instantiates P just in case a one-one mapping holds between some set or other of O's (possible) physical stimuli, inner states, and responses, and, respectively, the abstract input symbols, computational states, and output symbols tabulated in P. The intent of the NLA was to show that any such explication of a mental state-type would be far too liberal, since *if we are thus allowed to select any subset of physical states of O we like*, organism-program correlations of the sort just mentioned are trivially

easy to come by. In particular, Elugardo (1983; cf. also 1981), calling
my tepidly named O "Oscar" and my h "Harold," argues that if we
attend to what he calls "certain small and uninteresting parts of Oscar's body," viz., those parts that Oscar shares with Harold, we can
see that such a correlation holds trivially and parasitically between
Oscar and the program P appropriate for thinking that index cards
ought to be painted phosphorescently.

Elugardo questions whether "(Def.) does in fact specify a one-one
mapping" (p. 270) and doubts that "(Def.) does in fact show . . . that
Oscar realizes a Turing Machine program in the way that [I, WGL,
describe] a Turing Machine realization" (p. 271). Since the NLA
shows precisely that a one-one mapping holds between some of Oscar's physical states and the relevant constituents of P, I think Elugardo has conflated this issue with the other, quite different question
he raises in the same breath, that of whether "Machine Functionalism" as I have defined it has ever been held as such by any actual
philosopher of mind. He complains that

> the physical correlate of the input-symbol that Oscar is said to
> receive is not a physical input that Oscar *himself characteristically*
> receives; but rather, it is the physical input that Harold charac-
> teristically receives. . . . Surely this is not what the MFist has in
> mind when he speaks of machine realization . . . [W]hat counts
> as a physical input (output, state) of Harold need not count as a
> physical input (output, state) *of* Oscar even if the former input
> (output, state) occurs inside Oscar. . . .
>
> A general requirement emerges [:] . . . The machine character-
> ization must . . . describe a correlation of the person's own *char-
> acteristic* inputs, outputs, and states with the relevant abstract
> symbols in question. (P. 272; italics mine)

In effect, Elugardo is proposing a restricted use of the technical
term "realize," according to which Oscar does *not* "realize" program
P even though he does realize P in the sense I originally defined and
attributed to the "Machine Functionalist." The restriction is marked
by the words I have italicized in the foregoing quotation; Elugardo's
idea is to pick out a privileged subclass of Oscar's physical stimuli,
states, and responses and to count Oscar as "genuinely realizing" P
only if a one-one mapping holds between this privileged subclass—
Oscar's "own characteristic" inputs, outputs, and states—and the abstract symbols tabulated in P. Not just any subclass will do.

This restriction is intuitively appealing and does succeed in block-
ing the NLA. Moreover, it seems to block it in the right way; in my
view, what the Argument calls for is precisely a tightening of the

notion of "realization." But recall (as Elugardo does briefly on p. 273) that I deliberately defined "Machine Functionalism" in terms of the old, unrestricted, ultraliberal notion of realization, and so what the NLA shows is that MF (thus defined) is false and needs revision. Anticipating this rejoinder, Elugardo suggests that MF (thus defined) may well be a straw man. So it may be; early writers on functionalism were not very explicit about they meant by "realize."[6] The reason I focused on the unrestricted notion of realization (and so did not give the early writers the benefit of the doubt) is that the unrestricted notion is *clear*. Any attempt to tighten it up introduces obscurities and/ or unexplained primitives. Elugardo concedes in closing that his own term "characteristic" is a case in point. He does not tell us in any principled way which inputs, etc., are Oscar's "characteristic" ones (of course, we all know which ones he *wants* to pick out under that label). And it would be nice as well if he could give some independent motivation for singling out those particular ones—independent, that is, of the mere need to avoid the NLA counterexample.[7]

My own solution, compatible with Elugardo's and construable as a way of cashing it, will be to impose a teleological requirement (already heralded in Lycan (1981a,b,c). I shall characterize inputs, outputs, and functional states in job-descriptive terms, i.e., in terms that by their nature indicate the tasks their referents perform *for* the organisms in question. This relation of "for"-ness will yield a moderately clear and motivatable way of picking out Elugardo's "characteristic" inputs, outputs, and states, and thus will suffice to stymie the NLA. But teleological terms of this sort are notoriously troublesome; some philosophers suspect vitalism, some argue that the teleological notions logically require the pre-existence of an intelligent designer, some contend that teleological characterization is entirely subjective and interest-relative, etc. A theorist who follows my line on "genuine realization" buys into a host of serious problems, some of which will be addressed in the next chapter.[8] In the meantime I shall mention a few further examples to reinforce my point.

3. *Other Counterexamples to Machine Functionalism*

(1) (I owe this example to Ian Hinckfuss.[9]) Suppose a transparent plastic pail of spring water is sitting in the sun. At the micro-level, a vast seething complexity of things are going on: convection currents, frantic breeding of bacteria and other minuscule life forms, and so on. These things in turn require even more frantic activity at the molecular level to sustain them. Now is all this activity not complex enough that, simply by chance, it might realize a human program for

a brief period (given suitable correlations between certain micro-events and the requisite input-, output-, and state-symbols of the program)? And if so, must the Functionalist not conclude that the water in the pail briefly constitutes the body of a conscious being, and has thoughts and feelings and so on? Indeed, virtually any physical object under any conditions has enough activity going on within it at the molecular level that, if Hinckfuss is right about the pail of water, the functionalist quickly slips into a panpsychism that does seem obviously absurd; our feeling that pails of water, rocks, and piles of sand are not conscious cannot be diagnosed away as easily as Block's intuitions were. So it seems the onus is on me either to show that Hinckfuss's case could not really occur or to formulate Homunctionalism in such a way as to exclude entities of this sort from the community of sentient beings.

Note first that to counterexample Machine Functionalism the pail cannot merely ape the motions that are in fact made by some organism that is functionally organized on the human model, e.g., the actual goings-on in someone's CNS. It must also make all the input-output counterfactuals true, an unimaginably demanding task. If the pail actually were to do this, I would be inclined to suspect that it did have thoughts and feelings. But I grant that even this is not the real issue.

What I would like to say is that any even subjunctive "realization" of a human program by, say, H_2O atoms would be *fortuitous*. Relative to all normal (and some abnormal) purposes, the motion of atoms through the void is random, and the degree of randomness present at the micro-level, for me, removes any temptation to concede that Hinckfuss's quantity of water is realizing the relevant program in any interesting or useful sense. What is missing, I think, is the idea of functional *organization*, or organic integrity and autonomy.

Notice that Block's two cases are underdescribed in this respect. On the one hand, we can suppose that the Chinese (say) "realize" the human program entirely fortuitously, just in virtue of going about their everyday jobs, taking coffee breaks, casually conversing about their sex lives, and so on, thereby standing in bare one-one correspondence to some machine program. On the opposite extreme,[10] the Chinese might have been molded by some superhuman intelligence into a gigantic machine, within which individual humans are mere physical cogs that roll down chutes and drop through slots, etc., quite irrespective of their own life-plans or any other mentation. If the latter obtains, or even if the homunculi and the Chinese workers, respectively, are *cooperating* in a real sense according to a prearranged plan to translate inputs into ultimate outputs, then there is far stronger inclination to grant sentience or at least sapience to the resulting giant organism. But nothing of this sort is going on within the pail of water. If I am right in identifying mental entities with items teleologically characterized, we see at once why Block's group organisms, nonfortuitously construed, may be admissible as sentient beings but Hinckfuss's pail of water is unequivocally not: the homunculi-head and the population of China incorporate "ϕ-ers," groups of items whose function it is to do ϕ, courtesy of bureaucrats who are doing all the work; the pail of water does not contain "-ers" of any kind that is mentioned in a Homunctionalist program, precisely because it is not organized in the relevant way, even if the *de facto* motions of some of the molecules in the pail happen to ape the motions that would be made by an organism that *was* functionally organized on the human model. (Of course, the pail of water does contain "-ers" of various other kinds: microorganisms, the cells of which they are made, and the molecules, or "moleculers," which themselves (in groups) are busily realizing the "cell" programs.[11])

So far I have simply asserted that the pail of water is not "organized" in the appropriate way, and so my response is not conclusive even though it seems right. In order to vindicate my suggestion, we would need a theory of what it is for a physical entity to constitute a *system*, organism, or bureaucracy. But these are paradigmatically teleological terms; so what we really need is a theory of teleologicalness, and we needed that anyway. If, as some philosophers of biology contend, teleological notions are to be cashed in evolutionary terms—more on which below—then we shall have an even easier time distinguishing between humans, animals, group organisms, etc., on the one hand, and Hinckfuss's pail of water on the other, for there is a fairly clear sense in which things of the former sort and their capacities are products of evolutionary processes, but the pail of water and its microactivities are not. Certainly the former items exhibit a continually improving adaptation of means to ends, and the pail does not. However this distinction may eventually be spelled out, I think we can be confident for now that Hinckfuss's pail does not meet proper teleological standards for sentience and so is not a counterexample to Homunctionalism as I shall be presenting it.

(2) Suppose (following Dreyfus, 1979) we have written a program whose function is to draw pictures of biological organs, and in particular the program makes diachronic movies of people's brains; the program is an artist that draws from life. Sensors attached to a subject's head feeds information to the program, which ultimately produces a giant CRT blowup of the subject's total neurophysiological activity. Now, assuming that nothing is broken and that the brain

activity is accurately scanned by the sensors and that the program's drawing is eventually written to the screen without error, there will be a lawlike one-one correspondence between the subject's brain events and the microelectronic events taking place in the screen; and the relevant counterfactuals will be sustained as well. (By "the microelectronic events" I mean, not the brain activity depicted on and by the screen, but those events *in* the CRT that do the depicting.) Thus in the MFist sense of counterfactual one-one correspondence, the screen realizes whatever program(s) the brain does. Yet no one would grant that the screen itself is conscious. I shall argue that this is because no event in the screen has a human type of function with respect to any other screen event or to the screen itself.

(3) Consider a case adapted by Block (1981a) from Searle (1980). A single homunculus sits inside a room that is fitted with input- and output-gates. The homunculus has been provided with a manual that codifies the program of a conscious being—say, that of a native speaker of Chinese. Upon receiving inputs to the room as a whole, working at high speed, the homunculus looks through his manual and with pencil and paper calculates the appropriate output and other functional effects, then implementing them by pulling levers or the like. No one would suggest that the homunculus understands Chinese, has a conscious mental life corresponding to the program expressed in the manual, or anything like that. Yet as before the program is being "realized" in the bare sense of MF.

It is now time to adumbrate my teleological hypothesis in considerably more detail; that will be the task of the next chapter.

Chapter 4

The Continuity of Levels of Nature

Contemporary Functionalism in the philosophy of mind began with a distinction between *role* and *occupant*. As we have seen, the seductive comparison of people (or their brains) to computing machines drew our attention to the contrast between a machine's program (abstractly viewed) and the particular stuff of which the machine happens to be physically made, that *realizes* the program. It is the former, not the latter, that interests us *vis-à-vis* the interpretation, explanation, prediction, and exploitation of the machine's "behavior"; people build computers to run programs, and use whatever physical materials will best lend themselves to that task.

The distinction between "program" and "realizing-stuff," or more familiarly "software" and "hardware," lent itself happily back to the philosophy of mind when Putnam and Fodor exposed the chauvinistic implications of the Identity Theory. What "c-fibers" and the like are doing could have been done—this role could have been performed—by some physiochemically different structure. And sure enough, if the same role were performed, the same functions realized, by silicon- instead of carbon-based neurochemistry, or if our individual neurons were replaced piecemeal by electronic prostheses that did the same jobs, then intuitively our mentality would remain unaffected. What matters is function, not functionary; program, not realizing-stuff; software, not hardware; role, not occupant. Thus the birth of Functionalism, and the distinction between "functional" and "structural" states or properties of an organism.

Functionalism is the only positive doctrine in all of philosophy that I am prepared (if not licensed) to kill for.[1] And I see the "role"/"occupant" distinction (some say obsessively) as fundamental to metaphysics. But I maintain that the *implementation* of that distinction in recent philosophy of mind is both wrong and pernicious. And my purpose in this chapter is to attack the dichotomies of "software"/ "hardware," "function"/"structure" in their usual philosophical forms, and to exhibit some of the substantive confusions and correct some of the mistakes that have flowed from them.

1. *The Hierarchy*

Very generally put, my objection is that "software"/"hardware" talk encourages the idea of a bipartite Nature, divided into two levels, roughly the physiochemical and the (supervenient) "functional" or higher-organizational—as against reality, which is a multiple *hierarchy* of levels of nature, each level marked by nexus of nomic generalizations and supervenient on all those levels below it on the continuum.[2] See Nature as hierarchically organized in this way, and the "function"/"structure" distinction *goes relative:* something is a role as opposed to an occupant, a functional state as opposed to a realizer, or vice versa, only *modulo* a designated level of nature. Let me illustrate.

Physiology and microphysiology abound with examples: *Cells*—to take a rather conspicuously functional term(!)—are constituted of cooperating teams of smaller items including membrane, nucleus, mitochondria, and the like: these items are themselves *systems* of yet smaller, still cooperating constituents. For that matter, still lower levels of nature are numerous and markedly distinct: the chemical, the molecular, the atomic, the (traditional) subatomic, the microphysical. Levels are nexus of interesting lawlike generalizations, and are individuated according to the types of generalizations involved. But cells, to look back upward along the hierarchy, are grouped into tissues, which combine to form organs, which group themselves into organ systems, which cooperate—marvelously—to comprise whole organisms such as human beings. Organisms, for that matter, collect themselves into organized (*organ-ized*) groups. And there is no clear difference of kind between what we ordinarily think of as single organisms and groups of organisms that function corporately in a markedly singleminded way—"group organisms" themselves, we might say.[3]

Corresponding to this bottom-up aggregative picture of the hierarchical organization of Nature is the familiar top-down explanatory strategy.[4] If we want to know how wastes and toxins are eliminated from the bodies of humans, we look for and find an *excretory system* interlocked with the digestive and circulatory systems. If we look at that system closely we find (not surprisingly) that it treats water-soluble and nonsoluble wastes differently. We find in particular a *kidney,* which works on soluble wastes in particular. If we probe the details further, proceeding downward through the hierarchy of levels, we find the kidney divided into renal cortex (a filter) and medulla (a collector). The cortex is composed mainly of nephrons. Each nephron has a glomerulus accessed by an afferent arteriole, and a contractile muscular cuff to control pressure (the pressure pushes water and solutes through the capillary walls into Bowman's Capsule, leaving blood cells and the larger blood proteins stuck behind). Reabsorption and so on are explained in cellular terms, e.g., by the special properties of the epithelial cells that line the nephron's long tubule; those special properties are in turn explained in terms of the physical chemistry of the cell membranes.

The brain is no exception to this hierarchical picture of the organism and its organs. *Neurons* are cells, comprised of *somata* containing a nucleus and protoplasm, and fibers attached to those somata, which fibers have rather dramatically isolable functions; and we are told even of smaller functional items such as the ionic pumps, which maintain high potassium concentration inside. Neurons themselves are grouped into nerve nets and other structures, such as columnar formations, which in turn combine to form larger, more clearly functional (though not so obviously modular) parts of the brain. The auditory system is a fair example. There is evidence that the auditory *cortex* displays two-dimensional columnar organization:[5] columns of variously specialized cells arranged along one axis respond selectively to frequencies indicated by incoming impulses from the auditory nerve, while columns roughly orthogonal to these somehow coordinate input from the one ear with input from the other. The particular sensitivities of the specialized cells is to be explained in turn by reference to ion transfer across cell membranes, and so on down. For its own part, the auditory cortex interacts with other higher-level agencies—the thalamus, the superior colliculus, and other cortical areas—which interactions are highly structured.

Thus do an aggregative ontology and a top-down epistemology of nature collaborate. The collaboration has been eloquently argued for the science of psychology in particular, by Attneave (1960), Fodor (1968b), and Dennett (1975). I shall develop the point at some length, following Lycan (1981a).

2. Homuncular Functionalism

Dennett takes his cue from the methodology of certain AI research projects:[6]

> The AI researcher *starts* with an intentionally characterized problem (e.g., how can I get a computer to *understand* questions of English?), breaks it down into sub-problems that are also intentionally characterized (e.g., how do I get the computer to *recognize* questions, *distinguish* subjects from predicates, *ignore*

irrelevant parsings?) and then breaks these problems down still further until finally he reaches problem or task descriptions that are obviously mechanistic. (P. 80)

Dennett extrapolates this methodological passage to the case of human psychology, and I take it to suggest that we view a *person* as a corporate entity that corporately performs many immensely complex functions—functions of the sort usually called mental or psychological. A psychologist who adopts Fodor's and Dennett's AI-inspired methodology will describe this person by means of a flow chart, which depicts the person's immediately sub-personal agencies and their many and various routes of access to each other that enable them to cooperate in carrying out the purposes of the containing "institution" or organism that that person is. Each of the immediately sub-personal agencies, represented by a "black box" on the original flow chart, is in turn describable by its own flow chart, that breaks *it* into further, sub-sub-personal agencies that cooperate to fulfill *its* purposes, and so on. On this view, the psychological capacities of a person and the various administrative units of a corporate organization stand in functional hierarchies of just the same type and in just the same sense.

To characterize the psychologists' quest in the way I have is to see them as first noting some intentionally or otherwise psychologically characterized abilities of the human subject at the level of data or phenomena, and positing—as theoretical entities—the homunculi or sub-personal agencies that are needed to explain the subject's having those abilities. Then the psychologists posit further, smaller homunculi in order to explain the previously posited molar behavior of the original homunculi, etc., etc. It is this feature of the Attneave/Fodor/ Dennett model that ingeniously blocks the standard Rylean infinite-regress objection to homuncular theories in psychology:[7] We explain the successful activity of one homunculus, not by idly positing a second homunculus within it that successfuly performs that activity, but by positing *a team* consisting of several smaller, individually less talented and more specialized homunculi—and detailing the ways in which the team members cooperate in order to produce their joint or corporate output.

Cognitive and perceptual psychologists have a reasonably good idea of the sorts of sub-personal agencies that will have to be assumed to be functioning within a human being in order for that human being to be able to perform the actions and other functions that it performs. Dennett (1978a, chapter 9) mentions, at the immediately sub-personal level, a "print-out component" or speech center,[8] a "higher executive or *Control* component," a "short-term memory store or buffer memory," a "perceptual analysis component," and a "problem-solving component." And Dennett (chapter 11) examines, in some clinical detail, a multilevelled sub-personal structure that models the behavior that manifests human pain. "Behavior" here must be understood very richly, since Dennett scrupulously takes into account, not just the usual sorts of behavior that are common coin among philosophical Behaviorists and the apostles of commonsense psychology, but subtler phenomena as well: very small differences in our phenomenological descriptions of pain; infrequently remarked phenomena such as the felt time lag between our feeling that we have been burned and our feeling the deep pain of the burn; and (most interesting from the Homunctionalist point of view) the grandly varied effects of a number of different kinds of anesthetics and other drugs on a patient's live and retrospective reports concerning pain. Considerations of these various sorts serve the psychologists (and Dennett) as vivid pointers toward complexities in the relevant functional organization of the CNS, indicating the distinct black-box components at various levels of institutional organization that we must represent in our hierarchically arranged flow diagrams—the kinds of receptors, inhibitors, filters, damping mechanisms, triggers, and so on that we must posit—and the comparably various sorts of pathways that connect these components with each other and with the grosser functional components of their owners such as perceptual analyzers, information stores, and the speech center.

The homuncular approach, teleologically interpreted, has many advantages. I shall recount them when I have said a bit more about teleology. In the meantime, I put my cards on the table as regards the general form of a type-identification of the mental with the not-so-obviously mental: I propose to type-identify a mental state with the property of having such-and-such an institutionally characterized state of affairs obtaining in one (or more) of one's appropriate homunctional departments or subagencies. (The subagencies are those that would be depicted in the flow charts associated with their owners at various levels of institutional abstraction.) The same holds for mental events, processes, and properties. To be in pain of type T, we might say, is for one's sub- . . . sub-personal ϕ-er to be in a characteristic state $S_T(\phi)$, or for a characteristic activity $A_T(\phi)$ to be going on in one's ϕ-er.

What exactly is the point of a mind, or the job it is supposed to do?

3. Homunculi and Teleology

It may be protested that the characterization "ϕ-er" and "$S_T(\phi)$" are themselves only implicitly defined by a teleological map of the organism, and that explications of them in turn would contain ultimately ineliminable references to other teleologically characterized agencies and states of the organism. This is plausible, but relatively harmless. Our job as philosophers of mind was to explicate the mental in a reductive (and noncircular) way, and this I am doing, by reducing mental characterization to homuncular institutional ones, which are teleological characterizations at various levels of functional abstraction. I am not additionally required to reduce the institutional characterizations to "nicer," more structural ones; if there were a reduction of institutional types to, say, physiological types, then on Homunctionalism the identity theory would be true. Institutional *types* (at any given hierarchical level of abstraction) are irreducible, though I assume throughout that institutional *tokens* are reducible in the sense of strict identity, all the way down to the subatomic level.

In fact, the irreducibility of institutional types makes for a mark in favor of Homunctionalism as a philosophical theory of the mental. As Donald Davidson and Wilfrid Sellars have both observed, an adequate theory of mind must, among its other tasks, explain the existence of the mind-body problem itself; this would involve explaining why the mental *seems* so different from the physical as to occasion Cartesianism in the naive, why it has historically proved so difficult even for the sophisticated to formulate a plausible reduction of the mental to the physical, and why our mental concepts as a family seem to comprise a "seamless whole," conceptually quite unrelated to the physiological or the physical family.[9] Homunctionalism provides the rudiments of such explanations. The apparent irreducibility of the mental is the genuine irreducibility of institutional types to the less teleological.[10] The difficulty of outlining a tenable reduction of the mental even to the institutional is due to our ignorance of the organizational workings of the institution itself at a sufficiently low level of abstraction. Nor is the irreducibility of institutional types to more physiological types an embarrassment, so long as our system of institutional categories, our system of physiological categories, and our system of physical categories are just alternative groupings of the same tokens.

Some philosophers might find the Homunctionalist "reduction" very cold comfort. Certainly it would bore anyone who antecedently understands teleological characterizations of things *in terms of* mental items such as desires or intentions. Of course, as the foregoing discussion implies, I do not understand teleological talk in that way; rather, I am taking mental types to form a small subclass of teleological types occurring for the most part at a high level of functional abstraction. But if so, then how *do* I understand the teleological?

On this general issue I have little of my own to contribute. I hope, and am inclined to believe, that the teleological characterizations that Homunctionalism requires can be independently explained in evolutionary terms. This hope is considerably encouraged by the work of Karl Popper, William Wimsatt, Larry Wright, Karen Neander, and other philosophers of biology;[11] I cannot improve on their technical discussions. However, I do want to make one theoretical point, and then offer one example to back it up.

The theoretical point is that the teleologicalness of characterizations is a matter of degree: some characterizations of a thing are more teleological than others. One and the same space-time slice may be occupied by a collection of molecules, a piece of very hard stuff, a metal strip with an articulated flange, a mover of tumblers, a key, an unlocker of doors, an allower of entry to hotel rooms, a facilitator of adulterous liaisons, a destroyer of souls. Thus, we cannot split our theory of nature neatly into a well-behaved, purely mechanistic part and dubious, messy vitalistic part better ignored or done away with. And for this reason we cannot maintain that a reduction of the mental to the teleological is no gain in ontological tractability; highly teleological characterizations, unlike naive and explicated mental characterizations, have the virtue of shading off fairly smoothly into (more) brutely physical ones.[12]

Let me give one illustration pertinent to psychology. Consider an organism capable of *recognizing faces* (to take one of Dennett's nice examples of a programmable psychological capacity). There is plenty of point to the question of *how* the organism does its job; the creature might accomplish its face-recognizing by being built according to any number of entirely dissimilar functional plans. Suppose the particular plan it does use is as follows: It will accept the command to identify only when it is given as input a front view, right profile, or left profile. The executive routine will direct a *viewpoint locator* to look over the perceptual display, and the viewpoint locator will sort the input into one of the three possible orientation categories. The display will then be shown to the appropriate *analyzer,* which will produce as output a coding of the display's content. A *librarian* will check this coded formula against the stock of similarly coded visual reports already stored in the organism's memory; if it finds a match, it will look at the identification tag attached to the matching code formula and show the tag to the organism's *public relations officer,* who will give phonological instructions to the *motor subroutines* that will result in the organism's publicly and loudly pronouncing a name.

Knowing that this is the way in which our particular face-recognizer performs its job, we may want to ask for further details. We may want to know how the viewpoint locator works (is it a simple template?), or how the PR office is organized, or what kinds of sub-components the analyzer employs. Suppose the analyzer is found to consist of a *projector*, which imposes a grid on the visual display, and a scanner, which runs through the grid a square at a time and produces a binary code number. We may go on to ask how the scanner works, and be told that it consists mainly of a light meter that registers a certain degree of darkness at a square and reports "0" or "1" accordingly; we may ask how the light meter works and be told some things about photosensitive chemicals, etc., etc. Now at what point in this descent through the institutional hierarchy (from *recognizer* to *scanner* to *light meter* to *photosensitive substance*, and as much further down as one might care to go) does our characterization stop being teleological, period, and start being purely mechanical, period? I think it is clear that there is no such point, but rather a finely grained continuum connecting the abstract and highly teleological to the grittily concrete and only barely teleological. And this is why the mental can *seem* totally distinct and cut off from the physiochemical without *being*, ontologically, any such thing.[13]

A final word about my reliance on barely explicated teleology: I do not claim that barely explicated teleology is good or desirable. I do not like it at all, myself. My point is only that the mystery of the mental is *no greater than* the mystery of the heart, the kidney, the carburetor or the pocket calculator. And as an ontological point it is a very comforting one.[14]

4. *Advantages of the Teleological Approach*

The reader will not have failed to notice that I take *function* very seriously and literally: as honest-to-goodness natural teleology.[15] The policy of taking "function" teleologically has some key virtues: (i) As we have seen, a teleological understanding of "function" helps to account for the perceived *seamlessness* of the mental, the interlocking of mental notions in a way that has nothing visibly to do with chemical and physical concepts.[16] (ii) By imposing a teleological requirement on the notion of functional realization, we avoid all of chapter 3's counterexamples to Machine Functionalism, and, I would claim, to any other version of Functionalism; see below. (iii) A teleological functionalism also helps us to understand the nature of biological and psychological *laws*, particularly in the face of Davidsonian skepticism about the latter (Lycan, 1981c; Cummins, 1983). (iv) If teleological characterizations are themselves explicated in evolutionary terms, then our capacities for mental states themselves become more readily explicable by final cause; it is more obvious why we have pains, beliefs, desires, and so on.[17] (v) The teleological view affords the beginnings of an account of *intentionality* that avoids the standard difficulties for other naturalistic accounts and in particular allows brain states and events to have *false* intentional content. Causal and nomological theories of intentionality tend to falter on this last task (cf. chapter 6, and see Lycan, forthcoming).

I have argued above that we need a notion of teleology that comes in degrees, or at least allows for degrees of teleologicalness of characterization, and that we already have such a notion, hard as it may be to explicate—recall the examples of the face-recognizer and the key. Philosophers may differ among themselves as to the correct analysis of this degree notion of teleology—for my own part, I tend to see the degrees as determined by amenability to explanation by final cause, where explanation "by final cause" is reconstrued in turn as a sort of evolutionary explanation (though some details of this remain to be worked out). But two main points are already clear: (i) At least for single organisms, degrees of teleologicalness of characterization correspond rather nicely to levels of nature.[18] And (ii) there is no single spot *either* on the continuum of teleologicalness or amid the various levels of nature where it is plainly natural to drive a decisive wedge, where descriptions of nature can be split neatly into a well-behaved, purely "structural," purely mechanistic mode and a more abstract and more dubious, intentional, and perhaps vitalistic mode—certainly not any spot that also corresponds to any intuitive distinction between the psychological and the merely chemical, for there is too much and too various biology in between.

My own panpsychist or at least panteleologic tendencies are showing now. Many tougher-minded philosophers will find them fanciful at best, and of course (in my lucid moments) I am prepared to admit that it is hard to see any use in regarding, say, *atomic*-level description as teleological to any degree;[19] certainly explanation-by-final-cause does not persist all the way down. *But:* Unmistakably teleological characterization (description that is obviously teleological to some however small degree) persists *as far* down as could possibly be relevant to psychology (well below neuroanatomy, for example). And the *role/occupant* distinction extends much further down still. Thus the vaunted "function"/"structure" distinction as ordinarily conceived by philosophers fails to get a grip on human psychology where it lives.

For that matter, ironically, the "function"/"structure" distinction applies in no unproblematic way to computers themselves. Just as the good old "analog"/"digital" distinction has been seen in recent years to be vexed at best,[20] even the "software"/"hardware" distinction *as it is literally applied within computer science* is philosophically unclear. (There is a nice paper yet to be written on this issue, entirely disregarding the philosophy of mind or Artificial Intelligence.) Note first that "software"/"hardware" does not (even *prima facie*) coincide with *"program"*/"hardware."[21] According to one current usage as I understand it, "software" is what is electronically alterable, paradigmatically *packaged* input such as is loaded into memory from a disk drive (or perhaps entered from the keyboard), while "hardware" is whatever is hard-*wired* or fixed in such a way that it can be altered only by physical snipping and resoldering inside the machine. *This* distinction (by whatever name) obviously does not coincide with the "program"/"realizing-materials" distinction, for what is intuitively and universally designated a *program* may be either loaded from without (as a way of structuring the previously "blank" memory) or entirely hard-wired *ab initio*. A non-"programmable" pocket calculator, e.g., uncontroversially *has* a program that computes arithmetical functions—calculators of different brands have different programs— but all these programs are hard-wired and unalterable from the keyboard; they are not "software" in the computer scientists' sense. Similarly, some computers have hard-wired programs corresponding to other brands' applications software: a dedicated machine might have Wordstar or some other word-processing program built in unalterably rather than loaded from a disk in the more customary way.[22]

Much more to the point, there is not, even in a particular computer, a single program that is *"its"* program; there is no one level of programming. We constantly hear talk, especially from philosophers of mind discussing functionalism pro or con, about a computer's *program* as opposed to the hardware that is realizing "it," but this is a misconception; in computer science—as in botany and zoology— there is a continuum or hierarchy of levels of organization rather than a two-levelled structure. Flipflops are grouped into banks and registers. In an 8-bit machine there are 2^8 possible settings in each unit, each of which can be expressed in binary machine code or alternatively in hex notation. A level higher, assembly language collects individual machine-code operations into often-used sequences and allows the defining of subroutines and the giving of function names; a *macro*-assembler introduces variables, affording a *library* of generically characterized subroutines (without knowing, e.g., the exact register locations that will be specified in machine code). A standard *programming language* such as BASIC or PASCAL or C can then be similarly constructed out of assembly language; PASCAL commands call sequences of machine-code instructions. Further programs are written "in" PASCAL or the like by the same aggregative process. And there are special-purpose and/or still higher-level languages (as they are happily called), including self-compilers and the like, based on the simpler and more general languages.[23] A programmer can program at whatever level suits the purposes of the moment. (I program, in an infantile sort of way, in BASIC, but there are people who work primarily in assembly language, and it is entirely possible though pointless and self-punishing to program directly in machine code; professional programmers, I am told, are likely to start a tiny seed in machine code or in assembly language and then bootstrap crazily through permutations of compilers and self-compilers.) But—to get to the point—which level of description of the machine's operation counts as "the" program, as opposed to the mechanical stuff that realizes "the" program, is entirely observer- and interest-relative. The question, "What program is the machine now running?" has more than one answer: "Do you mean in assembly language, in BASIC, in C, or in [say] PILOT?"—and the *preferred* answer will vary in context according to interests and purposes. My moral is that the absolute "function"/"structure" distinction, borrowed from automata theory by philosophers and then misapplied to living organisms, does not even apply to computers in the real world; there too, the distinction (though real enough) is *relative* to level of organization, though due to human artifice computers do not exhibit the same degree of physical modularity that organisms do.

Incidentally, there is an interesting terminological point[24] to be made about the coordinately contrastive expressions "function" and "structure" (which usage dates, I believe, from Putnam's "Minds and Machines," 1960): "Structure" is (when you think about it) a surprisingly organizational, I would say almost explicitly teleological, term; a *structure* is an organized collection of elements, somehow *held in place* and/or serving to hold other things in place for some purpose or other. It does not contrast markedly with "function," even though it is not synonymous with it (and even though "*a* structure" normally *serves* a function). How might we better express the notion of brute, primitive realizing-stuff that does or is supposed to contrast with the functional? We might try "functional"-as-opposed-to *purely mechanical.* "Mechanical"? Hardly—*mechanisms* are functional items *par excellence.* Purely . . . what? We are in search of prime matter here, or else perhaps Sartre's yucky grey dead matter. And that stuff, if there is any, can be characterized in either of only two ways: by contrast with the functional, at some chosen level of abstraction, as in "the stuff that cells are made of," or by direct reference to a specific kind of level-bound entity, such as molecules or atoms or quarks and gluons. In neither way do we succeed in isolating the desired *general* mode of purely nonfunctional characterization, the vernacular of *pure occupancy.* There may be "pure occupants" or prime matter, ultimate unrealized realizers, even *necessarily* fundamental particles—presumably there are, despite my own tendency to think that it is functions all the way down—but further descent is always *epistemically* possible for us, and so we have no ordinary word for pure occupancy. "Role"/ "occupant" remains a level-relative distinction; all we can mean by "pure occupant" is *stuff at a level L that realizes entities of level L + 1 but is not in fact realized at any lower level.*

Everything I have said so far may seem dull and obvious. I hope it does. I am trying to call attention to what I consider a home truth about the structure of the physical world, because I think neglect of this truth, inattention to the hierarchical nature of Nature, has led to significant errors and confusions about consciousness and "qualia." In the next chapter I shall review some of these and try to correct them.

Chapter 5

Homunctionalism and "Qualia"

I now turn to some problems concerning felt phenomenal characters, and offer solutions. I shall discuss some "qualia"-based objections that have been raised against standard Functionalist theories, and show that my version of Homunctionalism avoids them in what I think is an illuminating way.

1. Preliminaries

In chapter 1 I construed Putnam as accusing the Identity Theorist of overreacting to the Behaviorist's difficulties in allowing for the innerness and introspectibility of qualitative mental states. Fodor and Block (1972) made, in effect, a counteraccusation: that Putnam himself overreacted to the Identity Theorists' excesses and moved too far back toward Behaviorism. Since Functionalists characterize mental types in purely relational terms, they are unable to account for the purely monadic qualitative natures of those states, viz., their phenomenal feels. Block's homunculi-head cases are designed to show that.

I have already observed that Block's cases will succumb to an independently defensible teleological requirement. But even without that substantive commitment, we can effectively defuse such cases, showing that seductive as they may be, initial intuitions about them are untenable and have no force whatever against Homunctionalism. To begin, consider an offsetting counterintuition, well expressed by Dennett (1978a, chapter 11): Rejecting the suggestion that we account for the feel of pain by positing an otherwise useless "pain center" in our flow diagram, Dennett adds,

> Suppose there were a person of whom our sub-personal account (or a similar one) *without the pain center* were true. What are we to make of the supposition that he does not experience pain, because the sub-personal theory he instantiates does not provide for it? First we make the behaviorist's point that it will be hard to pick him out of a crowd, for his pain behavior will be indistin-

guishable from that of normal people. But also, it appears *he* will not know the difference, for after all, under normally painful circumstances he believes he is in pain, he finds he is not immune to torture, he gladly takes aspirin and tells us, one way or another, of the relief it provides. I would not want to take on the task of telling him how fortunate he was to be lacking the *je ne sais quoi* that constituted real pain. (Pp. 219–220)

The same may be said of a person suspected of being a homunculi-head, particularly when we remember the complexity and subtlety of all the variegated "behavior" that a Homunctionalist theory is determined to take into account. The case of the population of China is intuitively less vulnerable to this kind of appeal to our sympathy and fellow feeling, since, unlike the homunculi-head, it is not humanoid and, hence, does not so easily stir tenderness and pity. But if we were able to translate the Chinese giant's verbal or "verbal" output well enough to engage it in conversation and philosophical discussion, the same point could be made: we would have a hard time persuading it that there was something forever inaccessible to it that we have no means of conveying to it or causing in it, or (worse) that despite all its protests there is "nothing it is like to be" it. At best, it seems to me, we would have to concede that, although, the giant is not really in pain, it thinks it is, and this belief is entirely unshakable though utterly false.[1] To this extent at least, Block's case as *he* describes it is bizarre, and this bizarreness dims its appeal considerably, at least for me.

2. *Diagnosis*

If I am right in maintaining that Block's intuition is simply mistaken, what accounts for the intuition in the first place? I suggest that Block and those who share his skepticism concerning our two group organisms are the victims of a kind of Gestalt blindness. But this takes a bit of explaining.

Let us begin by taking further note of the fact, which actually is hinted at by Block himself (1978, p. 293), that if his pejorative intuition were sound, an exactly similar intuition would impugn brain matter in just the same way that his own impugns little bureaucrats: Since a neuron is just a simple little piece of insensate stuff that does nothing but let electrical current pass through it from one point in space to another, you would think that one could not produce *qualia* by merely stuffing an empty brainpan with neurons. But as a matter of fact I could and would produce feels, if I knew how to string the neurons together in the right way. The intuition expressed here about neuron-stringing, despite its evoking a perfectly appropriate sense of the *eerieness* of the mental, is just wrong.[2] (Notice carefully that in saying this I am not assuming the truth of materialism. I am assuming only that the mental *supervenes on* the neuroanatomical, as even Descartes may have conceded. This supervenience is no surprise to Block; I am arguing that the supervenience of the mental on the psychofunctional should not be surprising either.[3]) Let me expand on this point.

Suppose that you were a little, tiny person—say, just ten times the size of a smallish molecule. And suppose that you were located somewhere within Ned Block's brain, perhaps standing somewhere in his left occipital lobe. What would you see? It would seem to you that you were standing in the middle of a vast and largely empty space. Occasionally a molecule (looking something like a cluster of basketballs) would whiz by at a terrific rate; sometimes you would see two or more of these clusters collide and rebound. Now suppose someone were to suggest to you that in fact you were standing inside the body, indeed inside the visual system, of a huge conscious being, whose body consisted just of the aggregate of all those basketball clusters, and that that being at that moment was experiencing a vividly and homogeneously red visual sensation, just in virtue of those otherwise inert basketball clusters' whizzing and bouncing around in the way they are. This would probably seem totally absurd to you, in just the way (I submit) that the example of the population of China seems absurd to Block. *And you would be wrong,* if Block were standing before a smooth red wall in good light.

Why would you be so prone to make this mistake? Why should the truth seem so absurd and unbelievable to you? Presumably because you would be too small to see the forest for the trees. You would be unable to see Block as a person rather than as an aggregate of inert chunks of stuff. Were you to move across the room, grow in size, and look back at Block, you would automatically undergo Gestalt shift, and (according to etiquette) exclaim "Aha!" Similarly, Block is too small to see the Chinese mainland's inputs and outputs, respectively, as psychological stimuli and behavior to which he could relate; were he larger he would be able to see the population of China as a person, with the aid of a suitable translation manual. (As Dennett has noted in conversation, it is not an aggregate of items that is the subject of conscious states, but the person whose body the aggregate constitutes.) In the case of the homunculi-head, I suggest, the same Gestalt failure obtains even though Block is not smaller than the organism;

Block's attention is focused on the hectic activities of the little men, and so he is seeing the homunculi-head as if through a microscope, rather than as a whole macroscopic person whose inner mechanisms are so finely articulated as not even to appear articulated at all.[4]

In diagnosing Block's intuition I have tried to show that it was to be expected even though it is wrong. If this claim is correct—if Block would have his elitist intuitions about the homunculi-head and Chinese-giant cases *whether or not* the homunculi-head or the giant were conscious—then the intuitions have no force whatever against Homunctionalism.

The Gestalt phenomenon I have described is *part* of my diagnosis of "qualia" madness. More contributing factors will be revealed in succeeding chapters.

3. The Cases

Despite the importance of the points made in the preceding two sections, we need not quibble over dialectic in order to turn aside Block's type of objection. For our teleological requirement handles the counterexample cases nicely. We have already seen that on the strongly teleological interpretation of Block's examples, the temptation to write them off as nonconscious is diminished. The New Lilliputian Argument succumbs as well: Suppose, for example, that Harriet is a group organism. (On my view we are all group organisms, but let Harriet be a homunculi-head of Block's type.) As we have seen, for any of Harriet's constituent homunculi h and for any machine program state S, if h "realizes" S in the Machine Functionalist sense, then Harriet does also; so Machine Functionalism entails that, if one of her homunculi is thinking consciously that broccoli is awful, then Harriet is thinking that too; and if another of Harriet's homunculi is suffering sciatic pain, then Harriet is too; and so on.

Now, the Homunctionalist employs a more robust notion of realization, and so is able to avoid this objection. By individuating mental entities according to what they respectively *do for* their owners, we are able to prevent Harriet's overdose of mental activity. For a physiological state of one of her constituent homunculi, though *a fortiori* a physiological state of Harriet herself as well, need not be performing that service *for Harriet*. A state of one of the little women in her head that helps to purify the little woman's blood need have nothing at all to do with Harriet's circulatory system. And the physiological device that serves the little woman as her sciatic nerve does not also function as Harriet's sciatic nerve. (Notice how peculiar it is to credit Harriet with conscious awareness of sciatic pain if Harriet's *own* executive routine had no functional or physical route of access to the source of the trouble.) Likewise: suppose the Homunctionalist locates the state of thinking that broccoli is awful as a state $S_i(\phi)$ of one's ϕ-er. Then our friend h must have a ϕ-er as a sub-sub- . . . personal component of herself, and her ϕ-er must be in state $S_i(\phi)$. But whatever more structural mechanism it is in *h* that serves as her ϕ-er would not also be serving Harriet as *her* ϕ-er. So it does not follow (as it did from Machine Functionalism) that Harriet's ϕ-er is in state $S_i(\phi)$ or even that she has a ϕ-er at all; the objection is blocked.

Hinckfuss's pail is ruled out also, as has been discussed in chapter 3. So too is our artistic CRT, for it is the victim of vertical causation: The microelectronic events in the screen have no functions with respect to each other (indeed, they do not even have horizontal causal relations to each other). Their functions are to depict bits of the human subject's brain activity; nothing more. (They do nothing *for* the screen itself.) Finally, Block's single-homunculus-head succumbs. Although the single homunculus has a written copy of the psychological flow chart in question, and makes certain motions with his pencil that ape the functional relations codified in the flow chart, nothing in the "Chinese room" as a whole actually has as its function any of the activities so depicted.

4. *The Problem of the Inputs and the Outputs*

In defending Homunctionalism against "absent qualia" objections, I do not mean to imply that the task of accounting for qualia is easy or trivial. Aside from all the monstrous technical and methodological obstacles facing the psychology of sensation, there are at least two philosophical reasons why a Homunctional theorist would have to do substantive, hard work in order to produce even prototheories of the feel of pain, of the smoothness of colored visual expanses, and the like. First, the Functionalist model applies paradigmatically to information-bearing, cognitive states that are rather obviously computational in character. To be sure, there are "wantings to say" closely associated with sensations and their qualitative features. But it is hard to imagine how one might give a positive account of homogeneous phenomenal characters by explicating them entirely in terms of mechanical information accessing.[5] This is not because qualia enthusiasts such as Block are still in search of an extraneous light bulb or traditional homuncular locum or personal ghost in the skull, as I think Dennett supposes (see also Dennett, 1982, forthcoming-b; I believe it is because Block and other philosophers quite naturally have a hard time seeing how such a thing as a sweet taste or a static, homogeneous expanse of phenomenal color, in what Sellars calls the "aesthetically interesting" sense, could be explicable in purely relational terms. And making sense of this possibility requires positive effort on the Homunctionalist's part.

The second reason why the friends of qualia are right to demand such effort is that even if Block's two hypothetical cases have failed to refute Homunctionalism, some problems of chauvinism and liberalism remain to be resolved. Whether or not Fodor and Block are right in suggesting that Putnam moved too far back toward Behaviorism in backing off from the Identity Theory, the Functionalist certainly bears the responsibility of finding a level of characterization of mental states that is neither so abstract or behavioristic as to rule out the possibility of inverted spectrum, etc., nor so specific and structural as to fall into chauvinism. Block himself goes on to argue that this problem is insoluble.

He raises the dilemma for the characterization of *inputs* and *outputs* in particular. Plainly, inputs and outputs cannot be characterized in human neural terms; this would chauvinistically preclude our awarding mental descriptions to machines, Martians, and other creatures who differ from us biologically, no matter what convincing credentials they might offer in defense of their sentience. On the other hand, inputs and outputs cannot be characterized in purely abstract terms (i.e., merely as "inputs" and "outputs"), since this will lead to the sort of ultraliberalism that Block has disparaged by means of his earlier examples, and also by means of new ones, such as that of an economic system that has very complex inputs, outputs, and internal states but that certainly has no mental characteristics. Nor can we appeal to any particular sorts of interactions of the sentient being with its environment via inputs and outputs, since in a few cases (those of paralytics, brains *in vitro*, and the like) we want to award mental descriptions to objects that cannot succeed in interacting with their environments in any way. Block concludes,

> Is there a description of inputs and outputs specific enough to avoid liberalism, yet general enough to avoid chauvinism? I doubt that there is.
>
> Every proposal for a description of inputs and outputs I have seen or thought of is guilty of either liberalism or chauvinism. Though this paper has focused on liberalism, chauvinism is the more pervasive problem.
>
> . . . *there will be no physical characterizations that apply to all mental systems' inputs and outputs. Hence, any attempt to formulate a functional description with physical characterizations of inputs and outputs*

will exclude some [possible] systems with mentality, and thus will be chauvinist.

. . . On the other hand, you recall, characterizing inputs and outputs simply *as* inputs and outputs is inevitably liberal. I, for one, do not see how functionalism can describe inputs and outputs without falling afoul of either liberalism or chauvinism, or abandoning the original project of characterizing mentality in nonmental terms. I do not claim that this is a conclusive argument against functionalism. Rather, like the functionalist argument against physicalism, it is perhaps best construed as a burden of proof argument. (Pp. 315–318)

I am not sure how detailed a plan Block is demanding of the Functionalist here, though I have agreed that, on a mild-mannered understanding of "burden of proof," Block's challenge is one that the functionalist does bear the burden of meeting. The question is whether this burden is as prohibitively heavy as Block seems to assume. And there are at least three factors that I think lighten it considerably and give us some cause for optimism:

First, there is a line of argument that offers at least some slight positive reason or natural motivation for thinking that the dilemma of chauvinism and liberalism (either in regard to inputs and outputs or in regard to the inner states that the Functionalist identifies with our mental states) does admit a solution. It begins as a slippery-slope argument. Block has stated the dilemma very uncompromisingly, implying that one's only choices are (a) to characterize inputs and outputs physiologically and be a chauvinist, or (b) to characterize inputs and outputs "purely abstractly" and be a bleeding heart. But this brutal statement of the alternatives overlooks the fact, belabored in chapter 4, that functional abstraction is a matter of degree. Purely physiological characterization is an extreme, lying at the lower or "more structural" end of the spectrum; "purely abstract" characterization is the opposite extreme, lying at the higher or "more functional" end. Notice that (as I hinted in discussing Hinckfuss's pail) there are characterizations that are even *more* "structural" than physiological ones are, such as microphysical ones, relative to which physiological ones are "functional"; similarly, there are really more abstract characterizations than "input" and "output" themselves, such as "transfer," "motion," or even "occurrence." If it is true, as it seems to be, that "purely abstract" characterizations and physiological characterizations merely lie near the two ends of a continuum of functional abstraction, then it is reasonable to expect that there exists some intermediate level of abstraction that would yield characterizations that rules out the Bolivian economy, the Abnegonian Galaxy, the microbiology of the Everglades and their ilk, but would make room for human beings, molluscs, Martians, and brains *in vitro*. The truth lies (as it so often does) somewhere in between, and, depending on which aspect of which mental state interests one, not always at the same spot in between either. Wait and see what resources will be available at various intermediate levels.[6]

Now, intuitively, many of the items that would figure in psychologists' descriptions of inputs and outputs, such as *sentences*, have highly significant structure for which our developed psychology would require some semantical mode of representation, and that system of semantical description might well help us articulate our needed intermediate level of functional characterization. In fact, I suspect that a great preponderance of the functional descriptions that would figure in the kind of psychology I am envisaging will be semantical description. I have several reasons for suspecting and for hoping this. (i) Jerry Fodor (1975) has argued fairly persuasively that the computational processes carried out by any interesting agency of the brain (in our model, by the person's subordinate homunculi), being computational, must be couched in some system of representation, and that this system of representation will need to share enough of the characteristic features of natural languages so as to count as an internal language itself. It follows that the inputs and outputs over which the computations are defined will have semantical structure of some kind, and that this semantical level of structure will be the level that is relevant to psychological description and explanation.[7] (ii) If we describe propositional attitudes such as beliefs and desires, and the inputs and outputs germane to them, in semantical terms, we will be able (à la Sellars) to understand the intentionality of the attitudes as being a special case of the intentionality of sentences, a move whose explanatory value has been considerably increased by the recent elaboration of causal theories of referring. We may also account for beliefs' and thoughts' having truth values, exploiting the recursion that we suppose effect the truth valuations of sentences of formal and natural languages. (iii) In trying to work out a homuncular map of the human speech center (Lycan, 1984a, chapter 11), I have come to think that sentential structures *cannot be created within the speech center itself*. If this is right, then (since the speech center *ipso facto* produces sententially structured items as outputs) it must antecedently accept them as inputs. But its inputs come largely from cognitive and conative components whose trade goods are beliefs, perceptual states, and other propositional attitudes. So it is likely that at least the beliefs and thoughts, and perhaps other states

among this group, are sententially structured. If the beliefs have semantical structure of some sort, then, as Fodor points out (1975, chapter 2), it is enormously probable that perceptual states also have
semantical structure, since otherwise we would have a hard time explaining how it is that perceptual states seemingly give rise directly
and immediately to beliefs. And so, finally, it is not unreasonable to
suggest that perceptual inputs and outputs *can* be characterized in
semantical terms of some sort even though we do not normally so
characterize them and may not immediately see how such characterizations would optimally be formulated.

It might be replied that even if overtly sentencelike inputs and outputs were to be represented in psychology as having characteristic
structures, economic events and the like are complex enough to instantiate those structures. Possibly so. But let us remember in addition (here is my second point in response to Block's challenge) that
nothing forces us to assume that all the different kinds of mental
states occur at the *same* level of functional abstraction. The intuitively
"more behavioral" sorts of mental states, such as beliefs and desires
and intentions, presumably occur at a relatively high level of abstraction, and this makes it easy for us to ascribe beliefs and desires and
intentions to Martians whose overt behavior and very superficial psychology match ours; the same is true of highly "informational" mental
activities such as remembering and (literal) computing. Intuitively,
"less behavioral," more qualitative mental states probably occur at a
much lower level of abstraction; sensings that have certain particular
kinds of qualitative characters probably *are* quite specific to species
(at least, we should not be very surprised to find out that this was
so), and quite possibly our Martian's humanoid behavior *is* prompted
by his having sensations (or possibly "schmensations") somewhat
unlike ours, despite his superficial behavioral similarities to us.

I am not aware that anyone has ever explicitly defended Two-
Levelism as such.[8] But Two-Levelism seems to be what lies directly
behind such apparent dilemmas as Block's "problem of the inputs and
the outputs."

Parallel considerations apply to the problem of intentionality. We
think that a state of an organism is either an intentional state or not,
period, and then we wonder what the functional or institutional locus
of intentionality might be. I do not think intentionality can be a *purely*
functional property at all, for reasons that are now familiar,[9] but insofar as it is, I think we would do well to admit that intentionality
itself comes in degrees.[10] The "marks" of intentionality or aboutness
are none too clear, but what does seem clear upon reflection is that
there is an intermediate level of functional characterization that offers

a *kind* of directedness-upon-a-possibly-nonexistent-object-or-type that nevertheless falls short of the rich, full-blooded intentionality exhibited by the human mind: At this intermediate level, we speak systems-theoretically of "detectors," "scanners," "filters," "inhibitors," and the like, meaning these terms quite literally but without actually imputing *thought* or what might be called "occurrent" aboutness. But I must leave the development of these observations for another occasion.[11]

Third, it might be profitable for us simply to stand by the "purely abstract" characterization of inputs and outputs, throwing the whole problem of chauvinism and liberalism back onto our characterization of internal states and events. There are so many possibilities, so many different levels of abstraction in the functional hierarchy as it applies to the brain (many of which overlap and cut across each other), that it seems quite reasonable to expect there to be, for each mental state-type, some middle way between chauvinism and liberalism—not necessarily the *same* middle way for each state-type. It is simply an error to think that all mental phenomena must be functionally located at the same level, or that any single mental state must be localized entirely at one level. Regarding the "more functional," *nearly* behavioristic mental states, perhaps we would not even mind admitting that an economic system or the population of China could have such states (say, dispositional beliefs), if it were to come to that. And possibly at the least functional end of the continuum there are even mental state-types of which the Identity Theory is true, though it is hard to think of any mental state that is as "qualitative" as that.

The foregoing remarks suggest a final additional response to Block's "absent qualia" arguments, one that I think is virtually conclusive. Earlier I characterized Block's intuitive disquiet over Functionalism as being a matter of feeling the incongruity between the relationalness of Functionalist explications and the homogeneous, primitively *monadic* qualitative characters of their explicanda; I gather that this incongruity seems to him absolute. Notice that evidently he has no similar objection to the Identity Theory; like any other materialist, he would simply charge the Identity Theorist with chauvinism and raise no further complaint. After all, one of the theory's main advantages was its ability to account for the possibility of inverted spectrum or other inner variation despite outward conformity. But if we also accept my claim that Homunctional characterizations and physiological characterizations of states of persons reflect merely different levels of abstraction within a surrounding functional hierarchy or continuum, then we can no longer distinguish the Functionalist from the Identity Theorist in any absolute way. "Neuron," for example, may be understood either as a physiological term (denoting a kind of human cell) or as a (teleo-)functional term (denoting a relayer of electrical charge); on *either* construal it stands for an instantiable—if you like, for a role being played by a group of more fundamental objects. Thus, *even the Identity Theorist is a Functionalist*—one who locates mental entities at a very low level of abstraction. The moral is that if Block does want to insist that Functionalist psychology is stymied by a principled incongruity of the sort I have mentioned and that a philosophy of mind that explicates mental items in terms of relational roles of instantiables cannot in principle accommodate the intractable monadicity of qualia, then one would have to make the same charge against the Identity Theorist as well, and this, I trust he feels no intuitive compulsion to do.[12] (In fact, Block lets that Theory cop a plea of species chauvinism overall, and even allows that it is probably true of some mental properties (1978, p. 309).)

There is an idea, brought on by blind Two-Levelism, that Functionalism differs somehow *conceptually or structurally* from the Identity Theory, in such a way as to incur different sorts of objections. As I have said, the Identity Theory is just an empirically special case of Functionalism, one that (implausibly) locates all mental states at the same very low level of institutional abstraction—the neuroanatomical. Thus there should be no purely conceptual or philosophical objections that apply to Functionalism that do not apply to the Identity Theory or vice versa, even if one is empirically less reasonable than the other. Yet philosophers such as Block have claimed to see such objections. If my doctrine of the continuity of nature is right, something must be wrong here; for neuroanatomical terms are functional and so relational just as higher-organizational terms are, albeit at a lower level of abstraction. If there is a principled incongruity between relational characterization and the intrinsicness of phenomenal quality, and if that incongruity stymies Functionalism, then it should preclude the Identity Theory as well.[13]

Consider a second example of such an objection: Block further contends that Functionalism is unable to allow the possibility of "inverted spectrum" or other types of internally switched qualia unreflected even counterfactually in behavior—unable in a way that the Identity Theory is not, since the Identity Theory is *made to order* for representing cases of inverted qualia. But if my reflections on the continuity of levels of nature are right, something must be amiss here. And something is. Just as it is easy to imagine undetectably switched *neurophysiology* underlying inverted spectrum (see again Lycan, 1973), it is easy to imagine a switching of functional components more abstractly described (though doubtless there are limits to this, and quite possibly one could not ascend to a very much higher level of abstraction and keep the inversion behaviorally undetectable).

The truth of the matter is obscured by a pragmatic ambiguity in the notion of "inverted qualia," an ambiguity that I think has lent Block rhetorical aid even though it is far from subtle. To wit, there is a hidden parameter: "inverted" *with respect to what?* (Compare the correlative relation of *supervenience:* supervenient on what?) Traditionally, "inverted spectrum" has meant (color) qualia inverted with respect to actual and counterfactual input-output relations alone. Either from duty or by inclination, Analytical Behaviorists and Wittgensteinians denied the conceivability of *that* inversion, but most people's ordinary modal intuitions have favored it, and Identity and Functionalist theories alike have accommodated it with ease; it has never posed any threat to Functionalism. What would damage Functionalism is the conceivability of qualia inverted with respect to i-o relations *plus* internal functional organization. *This* inversion hypothesis is much stronger and more daring. Its possibility is controversial to say the least. Indeed, to assert it is simply to deny the truth of Functionalism—it is to say without argument that two organisms could differ in their qualitative states even though they were exactly alike in their entire global functional organization, *at whatever level of institutional abstraction is in question.* Of course there have been philosophers who have insisted without argument on the metaphysical possibility of organisms' differing in their qualitative states despite being *molecular* duplicates, for that matter, but such insistence has no intrinsic credibility even if the relevant theories of mind turn out in the end to be false. The possibility of spectrum inverted with respect to i-o relations alone is a well-entrenched and respectable though I suppose defeasible modal intuition; the possibility of spectrum inverted with respect to i-o relations *plus internal functional organization at however low a level of abstraction proponents feel it plausible to name* is anything but obvious and in conflict with some intuitively plausible supervenience theses.

(Some relationally minded theorists may find it natural to assume a certain *privileged* level of abstraction at the outset. For example, "*analytical* functionalists," or as I prefer to call them, commonsense relationalists, who hold that the *meanings of mental terms* are determined by the causal roles associated with those terms by common sense or "folk psychology," thereby deny themselves appeal to any level of functional organization lower than is accessible to common sense.[14] Folk psychology aside, the "High Church" computationalists[15] scorn appeal to human biology even within a purely *scientific* account of cognition and behavior, though their own chosen level of nature is none too clearly specified.[16] A theorist who cleaves to such a privileged level of organization may of course admit "inverted spectrum" relative to that chosen level, so long as he or she is willing to type-identify qualia with still lower-level items.[17])

[handwritten marginal note: "the difficulty with the qualia"]

5. Two Alternative Strategies

I have recommended one way of solving the problems of chauvinism and liberalism concerning qualia within a Functionalist ontology of the mental. There are alternative possible strategies. One alternative approach would be to bifurcate our view of the mental, by simply taking over the distinction between a mental state and its qualitative character, explicating the states in functional terms and the characters in rather broad physiological terms, tolerating the consequence that inverted spectrum or lesser interpersonal differences in qualia might be more prevalent than we think (viz., exactly as prevalent as are interpersonal physiological differences of comparable magnitude).[18] *[handwritten marginal note: "How can this work — it leaves the psychological completely unfixed."]*

Pain would present a useful test case for this second suggested way of accommodating qualia. An interesting and distinctive thing about pain is that (unlike most other mental states) it has both a strongly associated behavior pattern *and* vivid introspectible feely properties. This means, on the present proposal, that pain states may receive *multilevelled* analyses. For example (just to speculate a bit), we might end up wanting to classify any internal state of an organism that played pain's usual "gross" behavioral role (that of being caused by damage and producing withdrawal-*cum*-favoring) as being a pain, but to distinguish the feels of pains according to the states' physiological bases.[19] It would follow that, although mollusks and Martians have pains, their pains probably feel differently to them from the ways in which our pains feel to us. It would also follow that a state that feels like a pain state of mine might in a differently organized creature be a mental state of some kind other than pain; some philosophers may find this crassly counterintuitive.

Incidentally, the bifurcated view has become fairly popular in the past few years,[20] and is often expressed by saying that (e.g.) "pain itself is functional while its specific feel is neurophysiological." But the latter formulation again presupposes Two-Levelism. See the "functional"/"structural" distinction as level-relative, and the bifurcated theory collapses into a pointlessly specific version of the thesis (which I hope will become a truism) that mental states and their qualitative characters may well not be explicated in terms of the same level of nature (in particular, the locus of qualitative character may be lower in the hierarchy than that of the mental state generically considered).

I emphatically agree with the latter thesis, as I have already indicated, but it is no competing *alternative* to Functionalism.

A third alternative approach suggests itself for the case of bodily sensations (though I doubt whether it could easily be applied to perceptual qualia). It is to suppose that feelings that seem phenomenally to be simple are actually complex and that the distinctive quale associated with a feeling of a certain type is really the coincidence or superimposition of a number of distinct, individually manageable homunctional features. I think this line, rather than that adumbrated in the foregoing paragraph, is the most plausible to take for the case of pain, because it is strongly suggested by the anesthesiological data collected and summarized by Dennett (1978a, chapter 11). What these data seem to indicate is that chemically different anesthetics and analgesics disrupt subjects' normal "pain" subroutines at different functional junctures, eliciting from the subjects quite different verbal reports of their effects. Of a group of subjects suffering pain of roughly the same kind and intensity, one subgroup given drug *A* may report that the pain has diminished or gone away entirely, whereas a subgroup given drug *B* may report that although they know that the pain is still there, they cannot feel it; a subgroup given drug *C* may say that although they can still feel the pain just as intensely as ever, they do not *mind* any more; and so on. That some of these reports sound funny to us (they would be pooh-poohed as "unintelligible" by some Wittgensteinians) naturally reflects the fact that the subjects' normal inner workings are being disrupted, and their normal inner experience of pain being altered, by the drugs. What the drugs seem to be doing is *splitting off components* of the subjects' phenomenal experience of the pain, by splitting off component subsubroutines of its rather complicated functional basis. And if this is so, it follows that our phenomenal experience of pain *has* components—it is a complex, consisting (perhaps) of urges, desires, impulses, and beliefs, probably occurring at quite different levels of institutional abstraction. If these components can individually be split off from each other by drugs, then we may perform a *Gedankenexperiment* in which we hypothetically take a suffering subject, split off one component of his pain by administering drug *A*, then split off another component by administering drug *B*, and repeat this process, eliciting reports as we go to keep track of how we are doing. It seems to me plausible to think that if we were to keep this up, disrupting one access pathway after another and eliminating the component urges, desires, and beliefs one by one, we would sooner or later succeed in eliminating the pain itself; it also seems that if we were to reverse the process—to begin restoring the pathways by withholding the various drugs one by one—the subject would necessarily come to feel the full-fledged pain again (provided his damaged tissues had not been repaired in the meantime). I believe this makes it reasonable to suppose that some (again) *multilevelled* proper subsequence of the relevant complex of functional goings-on is both necessary and sufficient for the occurrence of the pain, contrary to the spirit of Block's antiliberalism.

I do not know how to make a conclusive choice among the three alternative approaches I have described, or what sorts of further evidence we might seek. I have run through some of the options only in order to show that the Homunctionalist has fairly rich resources that can be brought to bear both on the dilemma of chauvinism and liberalism and on the positive task of accounting for qualia. On the basis of these resources I believe we are entitled to conclude that Block's pessimism about qualia is unwarranted.

Incidentally, I have been assuming throughout this book that people do in fact have mental states that feel certain ways to them—more tendentiously but equivalently, that the states really do have qualitative or phenomenal characters, however those characters might eventually be explicated. This apparently truistic assumption has actually been challenged, most recently by Churchland and Churchland (1981) and by Dennett (1982, forthcoming-b), who defend the *elimination* of feels at the expense of (anything even remotely approaching) common sense. (See also Rey, 1986.) I would (and do) feel justified in stiff-arming their arguments on Moorean grounds, especially since I am claiming in this book to provide a fully adequate positive account of bona fide phenomenal characters. But I think the arguments can also be rebutted even without appeal to common sense; I shall undertake that task elsewhere.

6. Homunctionalism against Commonsense Relationalism

The continuity doctrine seems to me to count against David Lewis' theory of mind as expressed in his paper "Mad Pain and Martian Pain" (1981).[21] Lewis thinks we must have a *disjunctive* notion of a mental state such as pain, because of two separately apparent possibilities: that of a Martian in whom the commonsense causal role of pain was subserved by something other than c-fiber firings (this is the humdrum Functionalists' point against the Type Identity theory), and that of a human madman who has pain (realized by c-fiber firings) but in whom the pains do not fit the normal human pattern of causes and effects—they are not connected to other states in such a way as to cause withdrawal from stimulus, repair, and/or favoring of an injured part, cognitive distraction, the desire that they cease, etc.

Lewis is led by these considerations to a byzantine analysis that relativizes pains to populations. According to Lewis (as summarized by me), X is in pain *iff:*

> X is in the state S such that S plays the role C relative to some population P that is "appropriate to" X,

where C is the causal role associated by common sense with pain and the following *prima facie* "marks of appropriateness" are in play:

(1) You and I ∈ P.
(2) X ∈ P.
(3) X is not exceptional relative to P.
(4) P is a natural kind.

Attending to various further puzzle cases, Lewis develops a weighting-schedule for these four criteria, according to which (1) is outweighed by (2), (3) and (4) taken together; (3) is outweighed by (1), (2) and (4) taken together (indeed, (2) and (4) together outweigh either (1) or (3) alone); and the like.

I feel a powerful tension between Lewis' two intuitions, that the madman is in pain and that the Martian is also in pain. This is not particularly because I find a disjunctive analysis of pain unnatural; it is more specifically because the disjunction here is inter-level. An int*ra*-level disjunction would not bother me very much, but I have trouble imagining that a state could be a pain of a particular qualitative sort in virtue of either having a certain low-level, "structural" nature *or* playing a much higher-level, very abstract role (viz., the "usual" or gross causal role). Let me illustrate the problem by offering two intuitive counterexamples to Lewis' hypothesis.

(I) Suppose there is a kind of pain, "K-pain," in humans that physiologically consists just in a certain electrical transfer from an afferent nerve into a neural net that distributes the initial charge and sets up currents in several other nerves, perhaps including an efferent one. (Functionally what is going on is that the neural net is activating certain beliefs and inclinations and so on.) Now the *mechanism* here (a "K-mechanism") is itself quite trivial: it is just a soft wire with a sort of cat's-paw on the end. We might surgically remove my K-mechanism, not replacing it with another or with any functional equivalent; then I would not be able to have K-pains. The surgeon might then take my excised K-mechanism and wire it back into my lower abdomen, if (say) he needed some wetware to convey an electrical charge from my pancreas to various points in my liver and kidneys. He could have used any old nerve-plus-simple-net, but just happened to pick up my discarded K-mechanism because it was sitting there after the previous surgical procedure. The K-mechanism now is *just* conveying charge, not conveying it to anything anywhere near my brain or having anything whatever to do with my beliefs or desires or intentional behavior or any other psychological activity. Lewis is committed, I take it, to saying that I still have K-pains (as in my shoulder) when my K-mechanism fires, since the state of having one's K-mechanism firing is still the state that plays the gross causal role of K-pain in the rest of my population. But it is just a stupid little current passing through a simple little wire! And it is in an entirely wrong part of my body; how could *it* alone constitute that character-istic feeling of K-pain in my shoulder?

For that matter, suppose my K-mechanism were similarly im-planted into another patient, and that I was given a device that would enable me to tell when my old K-mechanism was firing in that recip-ient and conveying charge from *his* pancreas to his liver and kidneys. On the occasions when I do know that current is passing through the K-mechanism, should I express sympathy? The recipient will of course deny that he is in pain, express astonishment that I should think he is in pain, etc., and all of these quite sincerely, since he is not aware of pain in any cognitive or conative sense of "aware." Yet Lewis seems committed to saying that nevertheless the recipient is in pain and feeling the pain and experiencing the relevant *quale*. It seems to follow that I should feel sorry for him (the recipient, not Lewis). Or does he not deserve sympathy, on the grounds that what calls for sympathy in normal humans is not the pain itself but the frustrated desire that it stop, which our lucky victim does not have? But now I have less inclination than ever to admit that he is in K-pain.

(II) Suppose that when my K-mechanism was removed, it was re-placed by a prosthesis, say an actual hard (but very flexible) wire with various different resistances at various points within it. If this artificial K-mechanism or K-mechanism surrogate were to do just the same job as an actual K-mechanism, then it seems (at least to anyone who has any functionalist leanings at all) that I would still be able to feel K-pain. Yet I would not be in the physiological state that serves as pain in humans, and there is no other actual population in which pain is realized by prostheses like mine. Perhaps there is a set of nonactual counterparts of me whose nervous systems are all made of flexible wires, and these Wire People comprise a natural kind. But the reader and I and Lewis are not Wire People, so criterion (1) fails; I do not belong to their population, since I am still human, so criterion (2) fails; and even if I did belong to it I would be exceptional, I should think, so criterion (3) fails.

I am sure Lewis does not intend these unwelcome morals to be drawn from his view. He wants to deny that K-pain is a functional state in the sense of being defined by its gross causal role, since it can occur without in fact occupying that role; but he wants to admit that K-pain is a functional state at least in that it might have been realized by a different wire, etc. And he would agree[22] that my transplant recipient is not in (K-)pain despite having his brand-new K-mechanism firing, because the K-mechanism is not even playing its accustomed "structural" role (= role in the neural diagram, = role at the comparatively low level of functional abstraction that is in question), much less having its usual gross causal features. This distinguishes the transplant recipient from the madman, whose c-fibers are firing and who is therefore at least in the appropriate "structural" state—appropriate, that is, *in context*, where the c-fibers occupy the right niche or neighborhood in the madman's wiring diagram and are connected to the right sorts of components even though some of the connections are nonstandard for the species. The trouble is that the K-mechanism does not have its customary functional role but nevertheless still seems to be functionally characterized—very puzzling.

The puzzle, I need hardly say, is another artifact of implicit Two-Levelism.[23] The K-mechanism is not picked out by reference to its gross causal role, but it is not picked out by its purely "structural" (cellular) nature either. To a Two-Leveler this is anomalous. But to a Homunctionalist who accepts my continuity doctrine it is entirely to be expected, for like most states, K-pain is functionally localized at a level of nature somewhere in between. It is a subroutine that usually plays its commonsensically associated causal role but need not, and that is realized in normal humans by a certain sort of cell-aggregate but need not be. This view nicely accommodates our intuitions about cases (I) and (II), without falling into chauvinism, and it accounts for our feeling that although a "madman" is possible in that pain might not have its *gross* behavior-causal role, a state must have at least most of its usual psychofunctional environment to be thought of as a pain. Lewis' madman/Martian intuitions are troublesome only when one has not thought of the options we have concerning the location of pains in a rich institutional hierarchy. There is no need for a level-spanning disjunctive analysis.

Two-Levelism also lies behind a very natural but unsuccessful type of objection to Sydney Shoemaker's argument against the possibility of "absent qualia,"[24] in particular Ned Block's celebrated counterargument based on his "absent fluid" example.[25] Shoemaker's ingenious reasoning runs roughly as follows: Suppose there were a case of "absent qualia" in Block's sense, i.e., suppose a state S_1 of an organism O_1 has *quale* Q, but a state S_2 of a second organism O_2 is precisely functionally equivalent (causally equivalent in all psychologically relevant respects) to S_1 yet lacks Q:

1. $S_1(O_1)$ & $Q(S_1)$ & $S_2(O_2)$ & $FEq(S_2,S_1)$ & $\sim Q(S_2)$. [Assumption for *reductio*]

Now, if O_1 is in S_1 and S_1 has Q, then presumably O_1 can and normally does know that it is in a state that has Q.

2. $S_1(O_1)$ & $Q(S_1) \rightarrow$ PresumK[$O_1,Q(S_1)$].

But if any causal theory of knowing is true, then it is at least necessary for X's knowing it to be the case that P for the state of affairs that P to be among the causes of X's belief that P:

3. PresumK[$O_1,Q(S_1)$] $\rightarrow$ CAUSE($Q(S_1)$,B[$O_1,Q(S_1)$]).

Therefore

4. $S_1(O_1)$ & $Q(S_1) \rightarrow$ CAUSE($Q(S_1)$,B[$O_1,Q(S_1)$]). [2,3]

And

5. CAUSE($Q(S_1)$,B[$O_1,Q(S_1)$]). [1,4]

But, if S_1 and S_2 are truly functionally equivalent in the strong sense asserted in 1, then

6. CAUSE($Q(S_2)$,B[$O_2,Q(S_2)$]). [1,5, definition of *FEq*]

But obviously, if S_2 does not have Q, then no belief of O_2's is caused by S_2's having Q.

7. *CONTRADICTION!* [1,6]

Thus 1 is reduced to absurdity and "absent qualia" are shown impossible.

Block subtly attacks the move from 1 and 5 to 6, contending that Shoemaker ignores the fact of "multiple realizability" that got functionalism started in the first place. Suppose there is a simple calculator made out of hydraulic components that works only when the right fluid is in its tanks. Multiple realizability guarantees that an "absent fluid" hypothesis is true: a second calculator might be functionally equivalent to the first and yet lack fluid entirely, because it is not hydraulic at all but made of silicon or clothespins. Yet we could not validly conclude that the fluid does not play the relevant causal role in the hydraulic device, for by hypothesis it does.

It is easy to see how Two-Levelism leads Block straight to this objection. Suppose that there is a hard-and-fast function/structure distinction for human brains, and suppose that the locus of a pain *quale*

is the "structural" or neuroanatomical: pain of that particular qualitative character is to be identified with c-fiber stimulation (thus human chauvinism is true for pain of that type). On these assumptions,
the possibility of "absent qualia" follows trivially from the fact of multiple realizability. Given that something other than c-fibers could have
realized a person's damage-avoidance-and-repair program, it follows
that that program need not have been accompanied by the pain *quale*
(= c-fiber stimulation) and that an organism could realize it without
having the *quale*. So something *must* be wrong with Shoemaker's argument, and the "absent fluid" example shows what it is: although
the fluid is playing a causal role in the hydraulic calculator, it could
(nevertheless) be absent in a functionally equivalent device because
there could be something else, say silicon or clothespins, to take over
the role by causing the relevant computations itself.[26]

But let us reconsider Shoemaker's argument and Block's objection,
against the background of my continuity doctrine. Continue to suppose that Block is right about the locus of a pain *quale*'s being neuroanatomical, i.e., that chauvinism is true of pains that feel like ours.
(Other species lacking c-fibers can have pains, of course, but not ones
that feel to them the way ours feel to us.) Now I have argued that the
Type-Identity Theory is just a special if counterintuitive case of Homunctionalism; no exception, the Type-Identity Theorist regarding
pain *qualia* is just a Homunctionalist who thinks that specific pain
qualia are determined at a surprisingly low level of institutional abstraction. Then our Homunctionalist explication of "Organism O is in
pain of phenomenal type *T*" will make reference to c-fibers, using the
term "c-fiber" in a job-descriptive way. On this view, what becomes
of Block's "absent fluid" counterexample? The example depended
precisely on regarding the fluid as "structural" relative to the higher,
"computational" level, since it is precisely a case of multiple realizability. But on our present assumptions, "c-fiber" is being used as a
functional (Homunctional, job-descriptive) term; our focus is no longer
on what higher (more abstract) functions the c-fibers are realizing,
but on their being themselves realized by aggregates of cells. So on
this interpretation Block's analogy goes wide. If pain of type *T* really
just is c-fiber stimulation, then what we introspect when we introspect pain of type *T* is c-fiber stimulation *per se*, not some higher computational state that happens to be realized by c-fiber stimulation but
could easily have been realized by something else. If our c-fibers were
replaced by fine wire, for example, our Homunctionalist theory
would simply predict cessation of *T*-pain because the relevant sub-
sub- . . . subroutines (involving c-fibers *in propria persona*) *were no
longer being run*. Block would not have a case in which the program

runs as always even though "hardware" had been exchanged in mid-routine. If "absent qualia" are possible *and what this means is,* "absent" *relative to actual c-fiber stimulations* now construed as part of the relevant psychological program, then in order to make his move against Shoemaker he must suppose that the *quale* of *T*-pain is located still further down, in whatever is in turn *realizing* c-fiber stimulation. And then we would just revise our Homunctionalist theory accordingly and reiterate the foregoing response to Block's argument.[27] This just illustrates again the arbitrariness of choosing a level of nature *a priori* and announcing that *it* is the locus of *qualia,* even though we can agree that very high levels (and hence Behaviorism) as well as very low levels (e.g., the subatomic) can be ruled out as lacking any prior probability whatever. Shoemaker's argument is unscathed.[28]

If my continuity doctrine is obvious as stated, it has not been obvious enough to some of our leading philosophers of mind. I hope the foregoing demonstrations will also serve to make Homunctionalism all the more attractive as a theory of the mental.

Chapter 6

Awareness and Intentionality

One thing that is often meant by "conscious" is consciousness or awareness *of* something. In this very short chapter I shall merely indicate the line I wish to take on the nature of that "of"-ness, since I have little to add to what has already been said by others or by myself.

1. *Awareness*

We are sometimes conscious or aware of objects or events in the physical world. The items may be present to our senses, or we may learn of them at second hand, through hearsay or other indirect evidence. Either way, we have a standard case of mental aboutness; the "of"-ness in question is the traditional "arrow of intentionality."

I favor a "language-of-thought" view of intentionality generally (Lycan, 1981c, 1985, 1987; Boër and Lycan, 1986, following Sellars, 1963a. 1967, 1973, Fodor, 1975, 1978, and Field, 1978). That is, I hold that to be in an intentional state is to host a mental representation, a brain state that bears a natural (causal and teleological) relation to the object represented, or in the case of abstract or nonexistent objects, to linguistic events that go proxy for them. The details here are notoriously tricky and need a great deal of working out, but there is no *special* problem about consciousness or awareness over and above the problem of intentionality as traditionally framed.[1]

Self-consciousness is another matter. Awareness of one's own mental states is an elusive business.[2] Theorists rightly distinguish different forms of inner awareness. For example, Dennett (1969, pp. 118ff.) separates "awareness$_1$" from "awareness$_2$": A person is aware$_1$ that P when a direct input to his speech center has the content that P (this is the sense underlying his ability to report a mental state directly and noninferentially), while a person is aware$_2$ that P when an "internal event" of his both has the content that P and "is effective in directing current behavior." (The latter seems entirely neologistic, since paradigmatically subconscious states can be effective in directing current behavior, but Dennett explicitly disclaims fidelity to any ordinary notion of awareness.[3]) Hill (1986) distinguishes "Basic Awareness," a casual, passive condition of believing one is in state M where one's belief happens to be based on actually being in M, from "Active Introspection," the deliberate scrutiny of the contents of one's phenomenal field by act of will. I shall adopt Hill's terminology, finding it closer to expressing the epistemic notions that I think lie behind philosophical uses of the term "aware."

Basic Awareness presents no special problem. It is simply a case of intentionality, where the object of one's belief happens to be a state of one's own mind. Active Introspection, however, requires attention, for it is not merely intentional but involves the will as well as special attention phenomena that are not very well understood.

2. Introspecting

As I said in chapter 2, I construe Active Introspection as a monitoring phenomenon. That is, I fall in with Armstrong's (1968b) notion of Active Introspection as self-scanning.[4] But I would add three observations. First, as you may expect and for all the same sorts of reasons that figured in chapters 4 and 5, I urge that the posited scanning devices be understood teleologically; it is not for nothing that the word "scanner" ends in "-er." To be actively-introspectively aware that P is for one to have an internal scanner in working order that is operating on some state that is itself psychological and delivering information about that state to one's executive control unit.

The second observation is that there are obvious evolutionary reasons *why* we should have scanners of the sort envisaged. Parallel processing, time-sharing, and hierarchical control, all vital to the fabulous efficiency of such complex sensor-cognition-motor systems as we human beings are, individually and together require a formidable capacity for internal monitoring. Mother Nature could not possibly have produced systems of the human sort without having endowed us with ranks and ranks of self-scanners. It would be amazing, miraculous, if we were to turn out not to have such devices or if they were not to figure in selective attention phenomena.[5]

The third, corollary observation is that Armstrong is both right and wrong when he remarks that "[introspective] consciousness is the cream on the cake of mentality" (1981, p. 55). He is surely right in suggesting that a vast preponderance of mentation is not conscious at all, and that even Basic Awareness is not conscious in the sense of involving active introspective scrutiny. But he is wrong in hinting, as I think he intends to here and there, that introspective consciousness is an epiphenomenon or pleiotropism spun off from basic psychological functions as perhaps an evolutionary accident. Introspective consciousness is no accident, even though it is special and (so to speak) statistically rare: As a matter of engineering, if we did not have the devices of introspection, there would be no *we* to argue about, or to do the arguing.

Hill (1986) has challenged the self-scanning or "inner eye" model of introspection (in favor of a competing "Volume Control" hypothesis due to Dennett, 1978a, chapter 11), and his objection demands at least some response. It is based on the premise that "[a]ttending to a sensation normally involves one or more *qualitative* changes [in the sensation]" (p. 15). Since "the Inner Eye Hypothesis implies that attending to a sensation is ultimately a matter of forming a representation of the sensation," the hypothesis can accommodate the premise aforementioned

> *only by claiming that the process of forming a representation of a sensation is itself a qualitative change.* It follows that the Inner Eye Hypothesis is committed to *two* levels of qualitative states. One level consists of sensations, and the other consists of the states of one's internal scanning device that count as representations of sensations. (P. 16; italics original)

Hill goes on to fault the hypothesis on grounds of simplicity, complaining that the duplication of levels is unparsimonious.

I have several quick replies to make, though the issue deserves more thorough discussion. (i) We need not grant Hill's premise in the first place. That introspection sometimes seems (e.g.) to heighten or intensify the sensation introspected may be entirely illusory; for the sensation might well have been just as intense all along without the subject's having noticed it to be so. (ii) Even if active introspection does change the qualitative character of sensation, this change may be simply causal and mechanical. Ammeters and other measuring instruments notoriously change the values of the physical magnitudes they measure; it does not follow that they are not measuring instruments. (iii) For the same reason, it does not follow that "the process of forming a representation of a sensation is itself a qualitative change." To *cause* a qualitative change is not to *be* a qualitative change. (iv) In view of my earlier independent retrodiction of selection pressure toward internal monitoring devices, I do not see why it is unparsimonious to posit scanners, even if something like the Dennett-Hill "Volume Control" phenomenon turns out *also* to obtain.

Thus on balance I think the self-scanner model is unscathed by

Hill's critique. But the matter of self-consciousness is far from settled; we have yet to take on Thomas Nagel's well-known claim that what he calls "subjectivity" is an obstacle to materialism and to Functionalism in particular.

Chapter 7
"Subjectivity"

Nagel (1974) argues that the mental is in a way essentially subjective, and for this reason escapes the materialist's net. In his title he asks, "What is it like to be a bat?"[1] and he claims that nothing in physics, neurophysiology, or any other science as currently conceived can answer that question.

1. Nagel's Argument

Nagel's paper mixes up a number of quite different "qualia" problems and so bears any number of interpretations. (In particular, note that his title question is badly formulated. The issue is not one of what it is like *to be a bat* generally speaking, but what it is like for the bat *to be having the characteristic sensation* that we may suppose is associated with the operation of its sonar echo-location device; call that sensation "S.") Here is the version of Nagel's argument I think is the most interesting.[2]

1. There is something it is like to be a bat having the sonar sensation S.
2. We know all the facts there are to know about the bat's physiology and about its functional organization. [Supposition granted to the materialist.]

But

3. We do not know what it is like to be the bat having S.
4. If $F_1 = F_2$, then anyone who knows F_1 knows F_2. [Suppressed; assumes simple factive grammar of "know."]

So

5. There is a fact F_b, viz., the fact of what it is like to be the bat having S, which is distinct from every physiological or functional fact about the bat. [1,2,3,4]

6. If materialism is true, then every mental fact about the bat is identical with some physiological or functional fact. (N.b., "facts" here are *tokens*, not types.)

It follows from 5 and 6 that materialism is false. Nagel himself backs off this conclusion for some reason, affecting to concede that materialism is presumably true but failing to understand "how materialism could be true." It seems to me that if Nagel succeeds in proving *anything*, it is that materialism is false, period. But I do not think that Nagel succeeds in proving anything.[3]

2. What Is It Like to Be an Unsound Argument against Materialism?

Let us first ask whether premise 3 is really true. That depends a great deal on how we interpret it, and as Hofstadter (1981) has pointed out, the expression "know what it is like" is a very elusive one. There are several simple interpretations that make 3 obviously but unhelpfully (to Nagel) true: (i) We do not *have* the sonar sensation S; we cannot ourselves feel S. (ii) We do not know what it is like to have S (we do not have cognitive access to S) *in the way the bat does*. Both (i) and (ii) are obviously true, but both are welcomed by the materialist. Of course I do not have S, because I do not have the relevant functional organization, and of course I do not know S in the way the bat does, because the bat can scan itself from inside while I remain outside (in just the same sense, I cannot know your sensations in the way you know them). These facts are so obvious and compelling that they may nudge our intuitions toward Nagel's and make us sympathize with 3 as written; but they are dialectically irrelevant, because the materialist grants them. If 3 is supposed to help establish 5, it cannot come to just (i) or (ii), but must mean something more substantive about a somehow inaccessible perspectival fact.

There is a more general diagnostic point to be made here. Sometimes antimaterialist intuitions are generated by a kind of failure of stereoscopic vision, as follows: With one eye, so to speak, we look at the gray, cheesy brain of someone who is in fact having (say) a visual impression of blazing red. With the other eye, we vividly imagine seeing blazing red ourselves. The two images do not match; they are totally different, totally incongruous! How then could *seeing blazing red* simply be a matter of unobtrusive goings-on in one's cheesy gray stuff? Preposterous.

Exposed to the light of day, the fallacy here should be transparent. *Of course*, as I have said already, seeing someone's brain in a state of sensing-blazing-red is nothing at all like sensing blazing red oneself.

Nothing ever said or implied by any materialist has even faintly suggested that it is. Moreover, the felt incongruity is just what anyone, materialist or antimaterialist alike, should expect. Therefore the incongruity affords no objection whatever to materialism, and to take it as impugning or even embarrassing materialism is simply fallacious. Let us dub this error "the stereoscopic fallacy," and try as hard as we can to avoid it.

Incidentally, Nagel's footnote 6 sheds interesting light on the locution "know what it is like." If we were to take that locution at face value, we would understand it as having something to do with *like-ness* or resemblance; but Nagel explicitly disavows that understanding. If "like" does not mean *like*, what does it mean?[4] We do have a clear interpretive option: Understand Nagel's indirect-question clause as being transformationally derived from what is really a bound variable representing a "that"-clause, the content of which "that"-clause is in part demonstrative. Thus, generally, "S knows wh . . . Fa" is really "$(\exists P)(\exists c)(S$ knows P and $P = \ulcorner Fc \urcorner)$," where "$c$" is the individual constituent of the relevant fact. Rocky knows who robbed the diaper service in virtue of knowing some fact of the form "x robbed the diaper service." Now, specifically, we might say, "S knows what it is like to be a bat having S" is really "$(\exists P)(\exists c)(S$ knows P and $P = \ulcorner$ To be a bat having S is like $c \urcorner)$." There would have to be some individual constituent of Nagel's funny fact F_b, which S was mentally referring to, just as there has to be an individual robber of the diaper service. And S's mental reference to that constituent would have to be (if Nagel is right) a reference that *only S could make*; otherwise F_b could be stated in the third person and would be logically accessible to science after all. This suggests that S is employing a *private demonstrative*, or a private name he has coined for some aspect of his experience. If this is the correct interpretation of Nagel's position, then, Nagel has gone into the "private language" business, and now must join Kripke in facing the (I think) very powerful anti-private-language arguments advanced by Dewey, Wittgenstein, and Sellars against Russell and others.

3. The Move to Funny Facts

We have already seen that if the derivation of 5 is to be valid, we have to read 1 and 3 in some ill-understood but very substantive and tendentious way. There is a problem about the inference-licenser 4 as well. 4 is made initially plausible by the factive grammar of "know": if "know" is just a dyadic predicate that relates persons to (things called) facts, then 4 follows by Leibniz's Law; if F_1 *is* F_2 and F_2 is known by S, then F_1 is known by S.

The trouble is that there are obvious and direct counterexamples to 4, at least if we accept the standard uncontroversial scientific identities to which Smart compared his view. The fact of lightning's flashing in the sky is just the fact of a certain electrical discharge's taking place, yet some people know that lightning flashed but do not know about electricity at all. The fact of water splashing is a fact over and above that of some H_2O molecules' moving in certain ways, yet some people know that water is splashing but have never heard of H_2O. This should, I think, make us doubt the simple factive account of the grammar of "know," and it vitiates premise 4. Insofar as knowledge has objects, its objects are not *facts* in the sense in which we have been using that term.

4. *An Argument against "Perspectival Facts"*

Now I want to raise the question of whether there *could be* perspectival facts of the sort Nagel seems to be talking about. Nagel's argument seems closely connected to the older issue of the alleged irreducibility of self-regarding propositional attitudes and the allegedly intrinsic perspectivalness of (say) my belief that *I myself* am in danger (I shall discuss the connection below). That issue too features "perspectival facts" in some form, and in various writings[5] I have inveighed against them scientistically, but without really giving an argument. Now I think I can give an argument.

What is a fact? Let us suppose a fact is a composite made of individuals and their properties and relations. To each fact there corresponds a true proposition. The proposition is a composite made of concepts—individual concepts and predicative concepts, Fregean intensions. Each Fregean intension can be represented in the standard intensional logicians' way as a function from possible worlds to extensions. (An "individual concept" is a function that, given a world, picks out the relevant individual for us at that world. A predicative concept is one that similarly gives us the extension of the relevant predicate at each world.)

We are not told the logical forms of a typical Nagelian funny fact, but we can suppose that its alleged intrinsic perspectivalness is located either in an individual constituent or in a property constituent. Suppose the former. Then Nagel is telling us that there is an individual concept that can be grasped and/or reported only in a first-person, perspectival way, and not in the third-person, objective way. An individual concept is a function from worlds to individuals. But *any such function is objectively describable,* or so it would seem. There are plenty of individual-constant functions that are too complex or strange for us to grasp, so Nagel's point about alien concepts still holds, but there is nothing intrinsically perspectival about functions from worlds to individuals; any one could be described by anyone who had the right sort of mental apparatus or brain wiring.

Suppose Nagel locates the perspectivalness in the property constituent of his funny fact. Then, again, there will be a corresponding function from worlds to sets of individuals, and any such function is objectively describable. So where is the perspectivalness hiding? It seems Nagel will have to eschew this powerful and effective way of representing the constituents of propositions and facts if he is to maintain the existence of perspectival ones, and that we should be loath to do.[6]

5. Events, and the Banana Peel, Again

Notice that in several spots (not directly connected with the argument reconstructed above) Nagel makes the slip into act-object jargon that I have attributed to Kripke (viz., everyone grants that sensations considered *qua objects* of mental acts would have all sorts of properties that nothing physical could have, if there were any such objects, such as sense-data; it is only sensations in the sense of sens*ings* and events of experien*cing* that the materialist (token-)identifies with physical events).[7] As we saw in chapter 2, Kripke's essentialist thesis is plausible for the case of sense-data and other putative mental objects, if anyone could show that such objects exist and thereby show *straightway* that materialism is false; but Kripke's essentialism is hopeless regarding *events* (since particular events have no clearly essential features). Nagel slips on the same Banana Peel. For example, on p. 164 he talks of taking a "subjective *viewpoint toward* our experience" [my italics], and on p. 166 he talks of "how [his experiences] *appear to*" him [ditto]. But experiences are not objects that present appearances to us and toward which we take viewpoints; they *are* appearings and viewpoint-takings. To say, scientistically, that psychologists and brain physiologists are moving toward better and better objective descriptions of mental facts is not to take the subjectivity out of the experience and replace it with objectivity, but is to push for better description of the experience as a whole, subjectivity and all. The subjectivity is immanent to the experiental event; that does not prevent us from describing the whole event objectively. Not that this is an easy job. Our Functionalist psychologist still has to explain what it is about such-and-such a functional state that makes its proprietor think of it as subjective and point-of-view-y. Some of this will be explained by the fact that our perceptual processors are *filters*; they take in and retain only a tiny and tendentiously selected fraction of the information that is available in a perceived object. People viewing a physical object from (in the strictly literal sense[8]) different points of view take in different, and all incomplete, bunches of information about that object. This is *part* of the way in which our perceptual experience of the object is subjective.

6. The Rest of "Subjectivity"

Perceptual experience represents. I would claim (following Armstrong, 1961, 1962, and Pitcher, 1971) that *all* sensation represents. To sense or to feel is to sense something under a representation. And a representation is cognate with a Fregean sense, a Russellian description, a Meinongian Object, or in some other way a selective set of properties. Unsurprisingly, different representations differ functionally or computationally from each other even when they are representations of the same thing.

I maintain that the seeming uniqueness of "knowing what it is like" is of a piece with the seeming uniqueness of self-regarding knowledge and other propositional attitudes, discussed by Castañeda (1966) and many others. The latter holds no metaphysical interest (Boër and Lycan, 1980; Lycan, 1981c; Boër and Lycan, 1986); though self-regarding attitudes differ functionally from other attitudes directed upon the very same state of affairs, they have just the same truth-condition, that state of affairs itself. Thus there is no extra fact, and particularly not an "intrinsically perspectival" fact, that is known, believed, or whatever. I know that *I myself* weigh 180 pounds, while you know only that WGL—as you represent him—weighs 180 pounds; but it is the same fact that we both know. Two schemes of interpretation are in play, a functional or computational scheme that distinguishes my knowledge of my own weight from your knowledge of my weight (those bits of knowledge having quite different causal roles in the two of us), and a referential or truth-conditional scheme that does not distinguish them at all.

To "know what it is like" to have such-and-such a sensation is likewise a functional rather than a referential matter,[9] assuming there is no logically private reference to the *quale* of an immaterial sense-datum. If you allude to the firing of my c-fibers while I complain of pain, we refer to the very same state of affairs. But our respective functional states that happen to result in our doing so are quite different. In particular, the functional state of the bat having the sonar sensation S is quite different from that of the zoologist examining the bat's neurophysiology—of course. Nonetheless one and the same fact is apprehended by both (so far as the bat does at all "apprehend" its having S, which we grant for the sake of discussion).

There are no intrinsically subjective or perspectival facts. Not facts that are the special objects of self-regarding attitudes, not facts of "what it is like." There are only various functionally or computationally different states of subjects that home on the same objective state of affairs in virtue of those subjects' occasional modes of situation in their *de facto* environments.[10]

Chapter 8
Color as a Paradigm Case of a *Quale*

Opponents of Functionalism urge that the bright redness of a color patch or the distinctive taste of a tamarillo are intrinsically monadic, and cannot simply be a functional or other causal relation between the relevant sensing-event and some physical input or the like. And some bolder spirits even deny that such colors and tastes could *in any way* consist in configurations of subatomic particles.

We have seen that although philosophers are wont to speak of *"the qualia problem"* for materialism, "qualia" objections are markedly diverse: Even after we have carefully sifted all the diffuse "qualia" rhetoric we find in the literature and discarded what is merely muttering and/or posturing, there are several importantly different antimaterialist *arguments* that fall under the rubric, which arguments must be addressed separately and assessed on their own distinctive terms. We can now also draw an important moral from the Banana Peel: that even after we have distinguished these arguments, we must disambiguate them, accordingly as they do or do not assign to "qualia" the traditional categorial status of *first-order properties*. Let me explain.

1. Phenomenal Individuals versus Adverbially Qualified States

"Qualia" as originally conceived[1] are properties of phenomenal individuals. On this conception, the exemplification of a *quale* requires at least the ostensible existence of a phenomenal individual (a paradigm of such an individual's bearing a *quale* would be an after-image's having the vivid, homogeneous color it does). Of course, no materialist admits the existence of phenomenal individuals.[2] So it seems that if a "qualia" objection is to avoid begging the question, the objection must be understood to employ a less specific notion of a phenomenal character—not that of a first-order property of a phenomenal individual, but a looser notion of "feel" or qualitative character as being only a mode of classification of mental states, events, or processes. Materialists have tended charitably to assume that "qualia" objections were intended in this second, non-question-begging way, and have proceeded to deal with them (thus construed) rather easily.[3]

But suppose an objector insists that his qualia *are* intended as simple properties of phenomenal individuals. The charge of question-begging is not after all so obviously sound. The objector would thereby beg, only if his materialist opponent had already made a significant case against the existence of phenomenal individauls. And few such opponents have done that.[4] Most materialists have simply relied on the bad press incurred by sense-datum theories in recent decades and taken for granted that no right-thinking persons believe in phenomenal individuals (given the availability of "adverbial" theories of sensing and the like). Thus it is still open to the "qualia" enthusiast to press a case based on the existence of phenomenal individuals. In fact, I think such a case is considerably more compelling than materialists have granted to date. I shall state one, first against Functionalism and then against physicalism *tout court*.

Type-Type Functionalism

"Consider Leopold's mental state at a time t that immediately follows the firing of a red flash bulb immediately before Leopold's eyes: Leopold is having a bright, intense, vivid, homogeneously green after-image. The Functionalist characterizes and individuates mental state-types entirely in *relational* terms, viz., according to their causal relations to stimuli, responses, and each other. But mental types are ordinarily individuated according to certain occurrent characters that they involve—e.g., having a homogeneously green after-image is one type of mental state that seems to constitute a natural kind—and these occurrent characters seem intractably *monadic*. How can the occurrent *greenness* of Leopold's after-image be explicated as being a relation between Leopold's mental state and any other thing, and how can its homogeneity, its green-*through-and-through*-ness, be accommodated by a relational account?" The Functionalist characteristically replies to this objection by denying the existence of the after-image, paraphrasing away references to "it" as being adverbial modifications of a predicate of sensing: "Leopold is after-imaging homogeneously-greenly." The Functionalist then gives some relational explication of the adverbially qualified predicate of sensing, which explication serves as a 'topic-neutral translation' of that predicate.

Token-Token Physicalism

"Consider again Leopold's state of having a bright, intense, vivid, homogeneously green after-image. Now, neither inside nor outside

Leopold's head is there any physical thing in the room that is green; therefore, the after-image is not physical, and Leopold's mental state cannot be identified with a wholly physical state of his body." The token-token physicalist characteristically replies to this objection by going adverbial, as did the Functionalist, and giving another relational explication of the adverbially qualified predicate of sensing. By refusing to concede the existence of any phenomenal individual, the physicalist is able to block the objector's inference.

The physicalist's and Functionalist's responses by now have knee-jerk status; any contemporary philosopher of mind thinks he knows what "going adverbial" is, whether or not he agrees that we ought to do that. But the first point to be made about this is that it is *not* clear exactly what the adverbialist is saying, because the exact grammatical relation between the predicate of sensing and its "adverbial" modifier is almost never specified.[5,6] This needs investigation, and we shall see that the investigation embarrasses the adverbialist.

2. Adverbialism, Syntax, and Semantics

It is clear enough to allege that "greenly" in "after-images greenly" is a predicate modifier being applied to a verb; the logical form of the appropriate full predication is

[Greenly(After-Image)](Leopold).

Now, what about the grammatical status of "homogeneously" in "after-images homogeneously-greenly"? It makes a complex predicate out of something to which it is applied, but to what exactly *is* it applied?

Homogeneity is sometimes described as being a second-order property.[7] But this is not quite right, since "homogeneous" is not applied to abstract singular terms. The property *greenness itself* is not homogeneous. What is true is instead that some (zeroth-order) things, including Leopold's after-image, have greenness homogeneous*ly*, which is simply to say that every (proper or improper) part of them is green. (If homogeneity is a *property* at all, as opposed to some other kind of Fregean intension, it is a property of property-instantiatings, whatever that might mean. And this strongly suggests that it also cannot be kicked upstairs and made into some still higher-order property in the way that the greenness of a zeroth-order object can be kicked upstairs and made into an adverbial property of a mental act-property.) So we should not describe Leopold's plight "adverbially" by saying "Leopold is after-imaging homogeneously-greenly," but rather by saying "Leopold is sensing a-homogeneously-green-patch-ly,"[8] the logical form of which is presumably written as something like

[(∃x)Homogeneously([Green(Patch)](x))(Sensing)](Leopold),

where again the square brackets are predicate-forming devices.[9]

The syntax of this version of the "adverbial" approach is now clear, but the semantics is not. How is one to compute the truth-value of a formula of this type? We do not even know what *kind* of adverb our new complex predicate modifier is, and so we have received no advice at all as to how to evaluate a subject-predicate sentence whose complex predicate contains a quantifier—our "adverbial" explicans is *undefined*, and so cannot provide the materialist with any aid and comfort yet. Let us see if we cannot come up with some suggestions as to how our new syntactic constructions might plausibly be interpreted.

The physicalist's adverbs sound like manner- or instrumental adverbs as much as they do any other kind, so let us try construing them on some such model. Does English contain any manner-adverb or instrumental adverb constructions involving predicate modifiers that have existential quantifiers as constituents?

Indeed yes. Consider "Leopold is buttering with a knife," which we may paraphrase as "Leopold is buttering with-a-knife-ly," where the adverb is understood as being a predicate modifier. The logical form of the latter will give the quantifier wide scope, since our original sentence entails "There is a knife with which Leopold is buttering":

(∃x)(Knife(x) & [With(Buttering)](x,Leopold)).

In general, adverbial constructions containing quantifiers extrude their quantifiers in this way (cf. Clark, 1970).

But precisely this extrusion feature prevents us from understanding adverbial sensing talk on the same model. For "Leopold is sensing a-homogeneously-green-patch-ly" is designed precisely *not* to entail "There is a homogeneous green patch that Leopold is sensing." We must seek a different sort of syntactic paradigm. Is there a manner- or instrumental adverb that does *not* extrude its contained quantifier in the way we have seen?

Again yes. Consider "Leopold is running as if a lion were chasing him," which we may paraphrase as "Leopold is running a-lion-is-chasing-him-ly." The logical form of this will *not* have its quantifier in wide-scope position, since the original sentence does not entail "There is a lion chasing Leopold":

$$[((\exists x)(Lion(x) \text{ \& } Chasing(x, Leopold)))\text{-ly}(Running)](Leopold).$$

The parallel analysis of "Leopold is sensing a-homogeneously-green-patch-ly" is

$$[((\exists x)(Homogeneously([Green(Patch)](x)) \text{ \& } Present\text{-to}(x, Leopold)))\text{-ly}(Sensing)](Leopold),$$

which we may render colloquially as "Leopold is sensing as if a green patch were present to him."

This colloquialism has a familiar ring. Notice that "as if" is elliptical: "Leopold is running as if a lion were chasing him" is short for "Leopold is running as *he would be running* if a lion were chasing him." If we pursue our parallel analysis, we must regard "Leopold is sensing as if a green patch were present to him" as elliptical for "Leopold is sensing as *he would be sensing* if a green patch were present to him," and this explication is as near as anyone might wish to "Leopold is in that state typically brought about by the presence of a green patch in front of him," "Something is going on in Leopold that is like what goes on in him when a green patch is present to him," and their ilk. Thus, the "adverbial" analysis properly understood not only allows an Australian-style topic-neutral translation but *is* one.

However, we have yet to solve our problem concerning the quantifier. The original intent of the adverbial theory was to avoid quantification *tout court*, quantified variables having as they do a nasty habit of introducing entities even in a case such as this one, in which we want to say that no *entity* is involved save Leopold himself. Worse, the entity evidently introduced by the quantifier in the logical form displayed above is a *green* entity, and our whole project began when we noticed that no physical entity in or near Leopold is green. Nor have we answered the question of how the truth-value of the logical form is to be computed. But by understanding our adverbial modifer on the "as if" model we have made progress, for we can now buy in on standard semantics for counterfactuals.

We might use any going account of counterfactuals,[10] but the result will be the same: According to any such account nowadays, the antecedent of a counterfactual directs our attention to what is going on in a possible world distinct from ours. What is the antecedent of our Australian counterfactual? We may paraphrase the counterfactual as "There is a mode of sensing M such that Leopold is sensing in way M and Leopold would be sensing in way M if a green patch were present to him and conditions were normal." The antecedent of this counterfactual is "There is a green patch present to Leopold." Thus, any of the standard accounts mentioned above directs us to look at an alternative world in which (it is really true that) there is a green patch present to Leopold. And this is the source of our quantifier: the value of its variable *is* a green—physically green—patch.

3. *Phenomenal Individuals from a Materialist Point of View*

Thus we are after all able to agree with Frank Jackson (1977)[11] that contrary to the initial spirit of adverbialism, phenomenal description of our sensory fields is ultimately talk of individuals and their properties. Does it follow that we must accept sense-data? If so, then we need argue no further about materialism. Since a homogeneously green phenomenal individual is a nonphysical individual, as our opening argument involving Leopold asserted, we could not accept sense-data and maintain that only physical objects exist; moreover we would have to come up with some account of how human beings are able to acquaint themselves with nonphysical individuals, an account that would very likely entail that human beings are not entirely physical individuals themselves. Happily, however, there is a way out—a way of avoiding the consequence that there are sense-data.

I have agreed with Jackson's claim that homogeneous color is a first-order property of individuals. Fortunately, it is open to us to disagree with his assumption that the individuals thus colored must be actual entities.[12] On the account I have sketched, Leopold's green patch is not here in this room with Leopold, because it is not in our world, the actual world, at all. I take the view, defended by Hintikka (1969) and more recently by Robert Kraut (1982) that phenomenal individuals such as sense-data are intentional inexistents à la Brentano and Meinong.[13] It is, after all, no surprise to be told that mental states have intentional objects that may not exist. So why should we not suppose that after-images and other sense-data are intentional objects that do not exist? If they do not exist, then—*voila!*—they do not exist; there are in reality no such things. And that is why we can consistently admit that phenomenal-color properties qualify individuals without granting that there exist individuals that are the bearers of phenomenal-color properties.

A believer in actual sense-data such as green after-images may protest that he can *see* the after-image he is having, that it is right before his eyes, and that nothing could be more obvious to him than its actual existence. But how might the believer defend this last claim against the competing hypothesis that it merely *looks to him as though* there were something green before him, when in reality there is not? Indeed, that hypothesis seems a very fair description of what is going on. And we even have a well-worked-out physiological account of after-imaging that explains the illusion: it looks to Leopold as though there were something green before him because the visual processes that go on in him as a result of the flashing of the red bulb very largely overlap the processes that go on in him when he sees a genuinely green object under normal conditions.[14] There is no apparent reason why we should concede that the green thing he seems to see is actual.

If there were really sense-data, with which we were acquainted, there would be a serious question as to *how* we could be acquainted with them given that the notion of acquaintance is a causal one. The present idea avoids that question. To be "acquainted with" a nonveridical "sense-datum" is to represent a nonexistent object. There is of course a traditional and nasty problem of how it is possible to represent a nonexistent object; but that is a different, and quite general, problem.

Our homogeneity issue is at least temporarily resolved as well: The homogeneity of the greenness involved in Leopold's sensing greenly is simply the (in both senses) mundane homogeneity of the greenness of a physical object. This satisfies our insistent feeling that homogeneity is *essentially* a property of property-instantiatings and cannot be kicked upstairs.

As I said, we have arrived at (approximately) the Hintikka/Kraut theory of sensory objects. It should be noted that we have done so *merely by following the implications of the supposedly competing adverbial analysis itself* and not by theorizing along the lines drawn by Hintikka and Kraut themselves. This provides impressively independent confirmation of those theorists' views. Kraut's own discussion of these issues culminates in a *robustness* claim, to the effect that the same result emerges from each of two quite different lines of reasoning: the treatment of "phenomenal objects" as intentional inexistents, and the quite differently motivated Australian program of topic-neutral translation. I have now added a third, just as dramatically different route to the same analysis, via a proper understanding of the adverbial theory contrary to its originally purported status as a way of eschewing reference to phenomenal objects.[15] If robustness is a mark of truth, as I think it is, there is much to be said for the present treatment of "phenomenal objects."

4. Objections

At least four objections remain. One is of course a protest against my appeal to nonexistent possibles: Can a *materialist* invoke such things or "things," and even if so, why is that an improvement over sense-data or even Cartesian egos?[16]

A Lewisian realist regarding possibilia would not be embarrassed, for such a realist regards nonactual persons and objects as physical, flesh-and-blood entities even though they are located in worlds distinct from our own. But few philosophers are Lewisian realists, and in particular I am not one. For me (Lycan, 1979; Lycan and Shapiro, 1987) possibilia are abstract constructions, set-theoretic arrangements of properties and relations. My appeal to sets (and properties and relations) is indeed an embarrassment to physicalism, since sets et al. are nonspatiotemporal, acausal items, and physicalist arguments such as Armstrong's (1978a) can powerfully be wielded against them. Nevertheless, I want to say, sufficient unto the day is the evil thereof. Sets already and independently litter the philosophical scene, and are not specially dragged into it by my (or anyone's) theory of mind in particular. Eventually set theory will have to be either naturalized or rejected, if a thoroughgoing physicalism is to be maintained, but in the meantime I see nothing culpable about relying on them in addressing specific issues in other areas of metaphysics, and I do not see this first objection as serious.

A second objection is that free-floating sense-data do not always look like physical objects. If Leopold has been abusing some (nefarious) substance, he may be hallucinating in a way that involves filmy, free-floating shapes, swirls of color and the like, rather than Shakespearean daggers or pink rats. Thus the neighboring possible worlds may contain no physical objects in the ordinary sense that correspond to Leopold's chaotic hallucinations.

In fact that possibility is consistent with my analysis. For given any visual experience, it seems to me, there is *some* technological means of producing a veridical qualitative equivalent—e.g., a psychedelic movie shown to the subject in a small theater. Cinema screens are physical objects along with daggers and rats, and Walt Disney has left many heirs.

The third objection is this: I have said that the homogeneity of the greenness of a sensing is non-mysterious because it simply reduces to the homogeneity of the greenness of a physical patch (albeit a nonactual patch). But according to a proud tradition ranging from Protagoras through the British Empiricists to Sellars, the homogeneity of the colors of physical objects is unintelligible unless explained ultimately in terms of the homogeneity of the colors of sensings; on this view, physical objects are *not* (in reality) homogeneously colored, even in alternative possible worlds.

There is an irony here. Being found problematic when construed as genuinely inhering in ordinary physical objects, the secondary qualities were kicked upstairs into the mind, and made into properties of sense-data or at any rate modes of sensing. I now propose to kick them out of the mind, but not precisely back downstairs—rather, into neighboring possible worlds. Yet if the arguments against Direct Realism were good arguments in the first place, they presumably can be reiterated for the secondary qualities that inhabit worlds neighboring ours. It is not open to me to hold that at this world and those nomologically like it, a "green" object is simply an object that normally causes normal observers to sense greenly; to do so would close a circle of explication, albeit a slightly bent or twisted circle. Anyone who claims to solve the homogeneity problem in the way I have recommended must find some ground for rejecting Protagorean, Lockean, and Sellarsian arguments.

My own preference is to return to Direct Realism regarding the secondary qualities, despite the undeniable difficulties faced by that view, and to identify greenness in particular with some complex microphysical property exemplified by green physical objects. I am all but convinced by Armstrong's defenses of Direct Realism;[17] at least, I think there is a better case to be made for the combination of Direct Realism with my Krautian theory of phenomenal objects than there is for that of any psychological theory of the secondary qualities with a materialist theory of the mind. I cannot, of course, rehearse the cases for and against Direct Realism here.

The fourth objection is a bit tougher.[18] Even if lip service to Direct Realism is all very well, it seems I still have not captured the *homogeneity* of phenomenal greenness in particular. For even if Direct Realism is true physical objects are not homogeneously colored in Sellars' sense of homeomerousness—a green object has proper parts, such as electrons, that are not green. Therefore, even if "Leopold is sensing a homogeneously green patch" is to be explicated in terms of a genuinely green object at a nearby world, the latter object is not a *homogeneously* green object, and the adverb occurring in our target sentence remains unexplicated.

Note that the difficulty does not arise if we simply stick by our counterfactual formulation of the de-adverbialized analysis: "Leopold is sensing as he would be sensing if a homogeneously green object were present to him." For Leopold could be sensing in that way even if it is physically impossible for objects to be literally homogeneously green—the literal, through-and-through homogeneity of physical greenness would presumably not affect Leopold's visual response to confrontation by a green object. It is only when we cash the counterfactual formulation in terms of possible worlds that our third objection becomes a problem. Now, why not take seriously the suggestion that the nonactual objects I have posited are, unlike real physical objects, homogeneously colored?

To this it will be replied that the worlds inhabited by homogeneously colored objects would have to have very different physics, perhaps very different laws of nature, from those of our world. How could they then be regarded as "nearby" or "neighboring" worlds in the sense required by any going semantics for counterfactuals? I think this rhetorical question admits a serious and not implausible answer.

The problem of homogeneity begins with the notion that our Ur-concept of color *is* the concept of homogeneous color. Even though through science we come to find out that physical objects are not homogeneously colored, this discovery comes as a nasty conceptual shock, and remains anomalous even in the mind of so great a physicist as Eddington. Thus we may roughly distinguish two sorts of similarity or nearness relations defined on possible worlds: we might say, *nomological* nearness versus *conceptual* nearness. A world containing genuinely homogeneously colored objects is nomologically very remote from ours, as the third objector maintains. But if the Sellarsian point about our commonsensical way of conceiving color is right, such a world is conceptually very close to our own; in Hintikka-style jargon, only worlds of that type are "conceptual alternatives" for us, i.e., worlds compatible with the way in which we commonsensically conceive our surroundings. On most topics, our naive conceptions are themselves compatible with relevant scientific discoveries; the discoveries merely supplement and explain the commonsense beliefs couched in terms of the naive concepts. But as Sellars has always emphasized, this is dramatically untrue of color concepts—which is why color has seemed so intractable a strand of the world-knot. Thus it is not so surprising that the relevant conceptually-neighboring worlds should be nomologically remote, while the same is not true regarding other concepts such as those of the primary qualities.

André Gallois has raised a problem for the present approach to the problem of unhomogenous physics:[19] He draws our attention to the significant possibility that if the laws of nature were so altered as to afford the literal homogeneity of *objective* macroscopic color, then macroscopic objects might appear to us in unexpected ways. In particular, it may be factually the case that under such counternomological conditions a homogeneously green object would appear to us bluely or yellowly (or not at all) instead of greenly—thus falsifying our analysans.

This seems right, and I have no decisive reply to make, except to follow Gallois' own compensatory suggestion that our otherworldly green object might be more commonsensically characterized. Perhaps

instead of a (genuinely) homogeneously green object in a concep-
tually- rather than nomologically-neighboring world, we should posit
only a green object such that *any visible piece of that object would be green.*
In virtue of "visible" and "would," this proposal takes us to yet another range of worlds (ones in which parts of the green object are
both seen and green). But it meets Gallois' objection: if under normal
conditions Leopold were confronted by an object-such-that-any-
visible-part-of-that-object-would-be-green, he would sense homogeneously-greenly. Moreover, the proposal obviates our earlier need to
appeal to nomologically remote "conceptual" alternatives, since there
is nothing nomologically improper in its hypothesis. If it has offsetting defects, they can be left for another day.[20]

I pause to draw the moral that qualia *strictly construed* pose a harsh
and genuine challenge to materialism. And only in the foregoing way
or something very like it can that challenge be met.

Even the slightly desperate Hintikka/Kraut device cannot answer
one kind of antimaterialist argument based on the homogeneity of
color, due to Sellars (1956, 1963a, 1971). Let us turn briefly and in-
adequately to that argument.

5. Sellars' "Grain" Argument

Most qualia-based objections to materialism are easily refuted or at
least warded off. For this reason, materialists who do not notice the
differences between the objections may prematurely dismiss "qualia"
criticisms as a class, without noticing that some of the deeper criticisms have yet to be answered in any conclusive way.[21] The well-
known "grain" argument that emerges from Sellars' tireless struggle
with the homogeneity of sensuous color is one such criticism—perhaps the toughest of all.[22]

Sellars' examination of the "grain" issue begins in wonder, the
same wonder as that expressed by Eddington (1935) in his oft-cited
remark about the two tables: How can a homogeneously brown,
solid, immobile table be *identical* with a chaotic swarm of tiny colorless
particles moving at violent speeds through an almost completely
empty region of space? On the basis of what has been called his *first*
"grain" argument (Richardson and Muilenburg, 1982), Sellars arrives
at the view that the table's color is transcendentally ideal—that the
table is *not really* brown, even though by the language-entry rules
immanent to the Manifest Image[23] we are correct to call it "brown."
(Ultimate, real, or transcendental truth is truth-in-the-Scientific-Im-
age or truth-in-Peirceish, as opposed to truth-in-the-Manifest-Image.)
Determinate monadic sensuous colors, then, are not really in physical

objects. Sellars kicks them upstairs, Protagorean fashion, into the mind: what is true instead is that objects appear coloredly to perceivers. The table, more specifically, causes (most) people to have sense-impressions of a distinctive type, viz., that which Jones, who posited sense-impressions in the first place,[24] called the "of-brown" type.

So far, so good; but, Sellars observes, very little gain has been made against the general problem of homogeneity. For now the homogeneity of the brownness of the sense-impressions demands accounting for, and not merely as a property of some object in an alternative possible world. How can a sense-impression or perceptual experience *of* homogeneous brownness be a state of a thing (person) whose ultimate status in the Scientific Image is that of a chaotic swarm of colorless particles?

> [Eddington's] problem was to "fit together" the manifest table with the scientific table. Here the problem is to fit together the manifest sensation with its neurophysiological counterpart. And, interestingly enough, the problem in both cases is essentially the same: *how to reconcile the ultimate homogeneity of the [M]anifest [I]mage with the ultimate non-homogeneity of the system of scientific objects.* (1962, p. 36)

It would be a bad mistake, Sellars contends, to think that this reconciliation could be effected in any simple or straightforward way.

Sellars does not, as one might suppose, determine that his sensation or sense-impression is homogeneously colored by introspectively examining it and seeing that it is.[25] Adverbialism holds within the Manifest Image, he maintains; in that Image, a sense-impression is not an individual to which a person is related, but an adverbially qualified state of the person.[26] And of course, therefore, "the sense-impression" is not *literally* colored, since *states* are not the sorts of thing that have colors at all. Rather, the "of-brown"-ness of Sellars' sense-impression produced by the table is a property posited by Jones in introducing "of brown" as a (proto-)theoretical term within the Manifest Image,[27] and its homogeneity cannot be *perceived* in any way at all. We are forced to suppose that the "of-brown"-ness is homogeneous only because the theoretical concept of "of-brown"-ness was analogically derived by Jones from the ordinary Manifest concept of brownness, and homogeneity is a key element of the analogy that is the vehicle for this conceptual evolution. (Sellars is very rightly bent on keeping us aware that theoretical concepts do not leap into existence out of nowhere, but have to be developed in some way out of pre-existing conceptual material. His view is that they are derived from the ordinary concepts that figure in scientific *models*, by a gradual deforming that depends heavily on the preservation of analogical features throughout; it is in this way that the models turn into full-fledged and literal *theories*.[28] This account of the formation of scientific concepts is so plausible that one would have a hard time even thinking up a serious competitor; but it has some startling repercussions, as we shall see.)

So much for prototheory. What happens when we get serious and try to reduce persons and their states to swarms of tiny colorless particles, thus providing scientific cash in payment of Jones' promissory notes? We have to find something in the Scientific Image that actually plays the role marked in the Manifest Image by the term "brown sense-impression," and this something must be a state of a swarming aggregate, since such an aggregate will be the Scientific-Image counterpart of a Manifest person. Sellars is very wary of states of aggregates, for he is much concerned to avoid postulating *emergent* states and properties in what he considers an objectionable sense of "emergent." His policy is codified in his "Principle of Reducibility":

> If an object is in a strict sense a system of objects, then every property of the object must consist in the fact that its constituents have such and such qualities and in such and such relations. . . .(1962, p. 27)

Sellars is careful to insist in (1971) that this principle applies only within conceptual frameworks, not across them; the point is easily missed by the casual reader (and has been amply missed in the literature).

Now, what of the Scientific-Image counterpart of our brown sense-impression? Sellars' second and more famous "grain" argument ensues. The version of the argument that I shall discuss is not Sellars' own—at least, Sellars has vigorously disowned it in public.[29] Rather, it is the version that I think is the most interesting and powerful one that is directly inspired by his writings. In what follows I shall refer to it noncommittally as "Argument G." I shall be able only to sketch it in briefest outline. I begin with a passage from Sellars (1971):

> . . . the [Scientific-Image] successor concept of (visual) sensing is to define the ultimate home of the colors of the Manifest Image. And to do this job, it must relocate the "ultimate homogeneity" of the latter. But it cannot do so if the persons to which this successor concept applies consist of objects to which color concepts, in a sense which preserves the essentials of color space, do not apply. But, unless we introduce Cartesian minds as scientific objects, individual scientific objects cannot be meaningfully said to

sense-redly. Nor can the scientific objects postulated by the theory of inorganic matter be meaningfully said to be, in a relevant sense, colored. What is the alternative—if the principle of reducibility is not to be abandoned? It is, in the first approximation, to introduce a new domain of scientific objects to be the subjects of those successor color predicates. (Pp. 409–410)

Let me backtrack briefly and spell this out just a bit.[30] The analogy on the basis of which Jones formed his concept of a sense-impression, Sellars says, must preserve the "sensible quality dimension" of the Manifest physical objects that are the other term of the analogy; although sense-impressions, being states, are not literally colored, they are, let us say, quasi-colored,[31] and their quasi-colors are homogeneous. Now, the Scientific Image must contain a counterpart of our brown sense-impression, a theoretical entity that will take over the sense-impression's explanatory role. But the successor concept of that counterpart will be formed by the microscientist on the basis of a second analogy with the sense-impression, and that analogy too must preserve the "sensible quality dimension," on the same grounds as the first. Therefore, the sense-impression's Scientific-Image counterpart, presumably a state of a person-shaped swarm of tiny things, will have to be quasi-quasi-brown, and (again) homogeneously so.

How could a swarm or aggregate of tiny scientific objects separately have a state-property of this kind? Three ways come immediately to mind:

(a)   Quasi-quasi-brown-sensing might be an emergent state of the aggregate, in the sense of violating the Principle of Reducibility.

(b)   It might consist simply in the fact of the aggregate's physical$_2$ elements' being arranged in a certain way.

(An object is "physical$_2$" when it is specifically the sort of object that figures in the explanation and description of features of ordinary nonliving matter—the sort of object posited by current physics, for example (Sellars, 1971). An object is more generally "physical$_1$" if it is simply located in space-time.) Finally,

(c)   The sensing might be a state, not of anything physical$_2$, but of a little Cartesian ego that has found its way into the Scientific Image.

Possibility (a) has already been ruled out; and Sellars simply refuses to accept possibility (c). Possibility (b), though it would probably be the choice of most contemporary reductionists, fares no better: for physical$_2$ objects, particles by and large, are colorless, and according to Sellars no state that has the smoothly homogeneous "sensible quality dimension" could consist *simply* in the violent motions of a swarm of colorless particles, in the way a forest consists simply in an aggregate of trees. We teeter on the brink of paradox.

We are able to steady ourselves once we see that there is a further option:

> (d) Quasi-quasi-brown sensing might be a state of an aggregate, some of whose constituents are themselves quasi-quasi-brown (and which is therefore not physical$_2$ though it is still physical$_1$).

And this final possibility is that which Sellars prefers to any of the foregoing three. Therefore, he concludes, the Scientific Image will include some nonparticulate though physical$_1$ particulars which have quasi-quasi-sensible properties. He calls them *sensa*. Contemporary philosophy of mind has its Democriteans, its Empedocleans, and so on; Sellars is our only Anaxagorean.

6. *Sensa*

Sellars has profitably spent a good deal of time and energy attacking phenomenalist theories of several kinds; so one might be surprised to find him committed in the end to the presence of little (quasi-quasi) colored particulars in our ultimate account of the physical world. What *are* sensa, then, and how do they resemble and differ from the sense-data or "sense contents" of traditional phenomenalist metaphysics and epistemology?

The similarities seem to be the following: (1) Sensa are the things— particulars[32]—that (in the Scientific Image) are what actually have the sensible properties, or successor analogues of them, that physical objects veridically or nonveridically *appear* to us as having in cases of ostensible perceiving. Sellars maintains (2) that the "sense-datum inference" (exportation of the quantifier in a sentence such as "Robert senses *a red rectangle*") is *valid* in the Scientific Image (though fallacious in the Manifest Image); a red and rectangular sensum would be the actual object responsible for the truth of the wide-scope quantification. (3) Sensa are constituents of perceptual processes in our heads, and somehow function within us in such a way as to affect our beliefs and our behavior.

The most important difference between sensa and traditional sense-data (and the point to grasp first) is that neither in his adverbial account of sensing in the Manifest Image nor in his envisioned scien-

tific positing of sensa does Sellars award his perceptually basic entities the epistemological significance that sense-data have been
supposed to have. Sellars' purposes are purely ontological, and he
takes himself to have avoided what he thinks are the least plausible
components of sense-datum theories of perceptual *knowing*. In particular: (4) We have no direct epistemic *acquaintance* with sensa; indeed, it seems we bear no epistemic relation at all, at any given time,
to the sense occurring within us at that time.[33] (5) Sensa are (will be)
the highly theoretical posits of an esoterically developed microphysics, along with subatomic particles, fields, and the like. Accordingly,
(6) sensa are not discovered within the Manifest Image, either by introspection or by philosophical analysis of common sense; recall the
*in*validity of the "sense-datum inference" in the Manifest Image. Finally, (7) sensa are in physical, not phenomenal, space.[34] (They are
spatially located and, I assume, spatially extended.)

A few more characteristic features of sensa merit our attention: (8)
They are not particles, but they are just as basic to microphysics; they
co-exist with particles, and are just as real and just as substantial. (9)
Sellars hints in spots (e.g., 1962, p. 37; cf. 1981) that microparticles
and sensa will turn out to be (alternative) manifestations of an even
more basic common underlying sort of world stuff. (10) Though they
are constituents of the neurophysiological states that will be the
Scientific-Image counterparts of sensings, sensa play no role in the
explanation of the habits of nonliving things, and do not occur in the
systems of scientific objects that are the Scientific-Image counterparts
of nonliving physical$_2$ things (1963b, p. 105; Sellars and Meehl, 1958).

Sense-data were *mental* entities *par excellence*. Are sensa also mental? Well (I surmise Sellars would say), yes and no. The term "mental"
is amorphous and hides many important distinctions. As I have remarked, sensa are spatial, and so are not mental*istic* or Cartesian entities; they are physically located within their hosts' central nervous
systems. Are sensa "intersubjective"? Perhaps not in the sense that
they could be hosted by more than one sentient being at once; but
there seems to be no philosophical reason to deny that a sensum's
presence could be *detected* by someone other than its host with the
aid of some fancy microphysical measuring instrument. Perhaps a
decisive point, for Sellars, is that, being respectable scientific objects,
sensa are entirely actual and in no way "intentionally inexistent,"
thus sparing us the sorts of problems encountered in section 4 above;
nor is talk of them either intensional or inten*t*ional in Chisholm's way.
(Sellars regards the extensionality of sensa as crucial because he takes
irreducible intentionality to brand any entity that displays it as mental*istic*, as *"mental rather than physical"* (1971, p. 402).)

The anti-Cartesian tenor of Sellars' characterization of sensa is comforting, but it is hard to draw the wool over the steely eyes of a true
physicalist, however gently. Even if sensa are supposed to be the objects of a developed physics rather than ghostly ephemera, they will
seem very weird to the fashionably tough-minded philosopher who
likes the Democritean picture of the world and who expects the ca-
nonical properties of the ultimate microphysical simples to be expressed by final science in crisply mathematical terms. The suggested
addition of a predicate such as "quasi-quasi-brown," which (by stipulation) cannot sensibly be applied to any of the objects of current
microphysics, is intolerable to such a philosopher, especially when
we remember that colors are not the only properties of Manifest objects that have the homogeneous sensible dimension: some sensa will
not be quasi-quasi-colored or quasi-quasi-shaped, but will be quasi-
quasi-odorous or quasi-quasi-audible or quasi-quasi-tactile or even
quasi-quasi-itchy. Indeed, I think many people would insist on sight
that the conclusion of the second "grain" argument is simply incred-
ible and that both Sellars' own version and Argument G must contain
some error. To such people, Sellars responds as follows:

> . . . the [S]cientific [I]mage is not yet complete; we have not yet
> penetrated all the secrets of nature. (1962, p. 37)

> . . . what I find objectionable in the views of many of my tough-
> minded colleagues is . . . their failure to pay serious attention to
> the problem of specifying the conditions which an adequate
> scientific account of human behavior must meet. . . . This failure
> leads to a reliance on overly simple and inadequate paradigms
> of what will count as a "scientific object" . . . in this anticipated
> scientific account. (1971, p. 399)

> The important thing is not to let our reflections on the develop-
> ing Scientific Image of man-in-the-world be tied too closely to the
> current institutional and methodological structure of science, or,
> above all, to its current categorical structure. (1971, p. 440)

> Sensa are not "material" as "matter" is construed in the context
> of a physics with a particulate paradigm. But, then, as has often
> been pointed out, the more seriously this paradigm is taken, and
> the more classically it is construed, the less "matter" there seems
> to be. (1971, p. 446)

In short: It is not our place to second-guess the physicists. If we are
good Scientific Realists, we will not tie the physicists' hands by taking
it upon ourselves to tell them what they may or may not posit as their

theories develop and flower in response to encounters with new and even zanier microphenomena.

This is good advice, and if we *are* good Scientific Realists, we should follow it. Perhaps it is also a needed reminder to the tough-minded philosopher that he cannot *both* insist that he knows now what can and cannot figure as ultimate scientific furniture *and* play loyal squire to the forward-surging contemporary microphysicist. But I wonder if the (perhaps imaginary) author of Argument G does not have some need of this reminder himself. For, in arguing from his armchair that future science will have to posit nonparticulate sensa that have counterparts of the Manifest sensible qualities, is *he* not giving the microphysicists their marching orders in no uncertain terms? And might not a more properly obsequious Scientific Realist warn *him* to wait patiently for the scientists to let us in on what there is?

Probably the best way of exonerating Argument G from this charge is to understand it, not as handing out orders, but as simply *predicting* what physicists will in fact end up positing in their final account of nature. The prediction is based chiefly on Sellars' theory of concept-formation and conceptual change, and its apodeictic tone comes not from a dogmatic "first philosophy" or residual prescientific meta-physics, but from the fact that Sellars' account is the only plausible theory of scientific concept formation we have to date. I shall examine Argument G in this spirit, and see what else can be said about it considered as a prediction.

7. *Argument G and Science*

The first problem I see is the difficulty of surrounding the prediction with a scenario. How might it come about that *microphysicists* would be moved to posit sensa? Notice at the outset that microphysicists do not study human behavior, nor the neural processing of retinal signals, nor even the dynamics or kinematics of ordinary middle-sized inanimate objects. Their data lie at the molecular level, from which they peer unblinkingly downward. If a miniature microphysicist were to wander into your brain, in the course of his nature walk through the world, he would see excitingly complex organic molecules, but none that he could not see elsewhere outside the perimeter of a sentient being; acetyl choline is acetyl choline, inside or outside the skull, and the microphysicist's methodological apparatus certainly provides no way of discerning any difference. For this reason, I do not see how a *microphysicist* in particular could discover sensa even if they are demanded by some other (equally respectable) branch of natural science.

Of course, our reason for thinking that the microphysicist will have to posit sensa is not that the microphysicist will feel a direct theoretical need for them in approaching his own subject-matter, but that the microphysicist will be asked by the psychologist to find a state of his swarm of micro-objects that is playing a certain higher functional role, the role that is the Scientific-Image successor of the Manifest-Image activity of sensing in such-and-such a way. In particular, the psychologist is looking down at the microphysicist (from a higher level of functional organization) and telling him that he (the psychologist) needs some ultimate building blocks whose properties have the homogeneity that we ascribe to color properties in the Manifest Image. The Argument evidently assumes that the microphysicist will cooperate.

Cooperate in what way? We may assume that the microphysicist is tractable, but what resources has he? We have already observed that he has no methodological means of discovering sensa directly. The motivation for positing sensa (as Sellars himself reminds us (1971)) is the desire to help the psychologist, but there is nothing much the microphysicist can do *ex officio*. It sounds as though the psychologist is asking him for a personal favor, for altruism pure and simple: "I need some sensa—could I ask you to posit them for me?" There is no evident kickback or *quid pro quo*.[35]

It may seem odd that Sellars has located sensa in the domain of microphysics in the first place. If the need for sensa is the psychologist's need to begin with, why not let the psychologist do his own positing and spare him the slightly demeaning task of going begging in this way? In support of this, it seems that the area of our present scientific ignorance and naiveté that is most directly relevant to psychology is our ignorance of neurological structure and its higher functional organization, not our ignorance of microphysics. (Sellars' own example in (1971, p. 399) of the philosophers' handwaving term, "c-fiber stimulation," is an unwitting concession on this point.) Why is the second "grain" argument then not directed at the neuroanatomical rather than at the microphysical level?

The answer is that the objects of neuroanatomy—cells, principally—are composites, and are themselves reducible to composites at the molecular level. And so a reprise of the "grain" argument would have to be directed at them in turn; they, or their more advanced counterparts, would have to be at least partly composed of more basic objects that had quasi- . . . -quasi-sensible properties homogeneously, and so the neuroanatomist would end up hat in hand at the microphysicist's door even if the psychologist did not. Thus, it seems, we are stuck with our original problem: the microphysicist is being asked to make a commitment on behalf of his department that he has no departmental authorization for making. More generally, it is hard to see how one and the same kind of object can have both *just* those properties that future science will discover them to have, *and* the exotic properties that will be required of them in virtue of their role in Sellars' philosophical/psychological position (in virtue of their being the "ultimate inheritors" of the sensuous contents of perceivings), especially if those properties are supposed to be literally analogous to sensuous color, shape, and so on in the "aesthetically interesting" sense.

It is the crucial *monadicity* of these properties that gives rise to the present problem, in the following way: The onus of reduction is a top-down responsibility, not a bottom-up responsibility. As we know, a paradigm (which Sellars himself has done much to keep methodologically central) is role-occupant reduction, in which a practitioner of one of the special sciences makes use of a theoretical predicate that is a dummy or placeholder for whatever more basic object or system of objects will be found in fact to be playing a certain role. The role in question is normally a causal role; the special scientist looks at the syndrome of causes and effects in terms of which he has introduced his dummy predicate, calls down to the microphysicist (or to some other researcher at an intermediate level of organization), and asks him what more basic state of affairs it is that is brought about by those characteristic causes and in turn brings about the characteristic effects. All this is familiar to the point of nausea, but here is the problem: When the microphysicist or the neuroanatomist or whoever is asked such a question, he is normally able to answer it out of existing resources, to meet the demand with items already in stock. The apparatus of molecules-composed-of-atoms-composed-of-subatomic-particles-etc. is rich enough to provide the underpinnings of any sort of genuinely causal mechanism that a special scientist is likely to find in nature. The trouble with Sellars' intended reduction of Manifest-Image sense-impressions is that Jones' dummy predicates are not introduced entirely in terms of *relations* at all, but are forced (by Sellars' theory of conceptual evolution) to carry the monadic sensible-quality characterizations as well; so he cannot avail himself of the role-occupant model of reduction, at least not in its straightforward form. And this is why we are having trouble imagining how the methodological mechanics of the discovery of sensa could go. I will expand on this theme below.

Let me close this section with an argument loosely related to the foregoing. I am sure Sellars would like to reject at least one of the premises of this argument, but he has not specified which one and why: (1) Molecular facts supervene on microphysical facts of the sort that are fairly well-known even now in 1987. (After all, molecules are made straightforwardly of atoms, and atoms are composed *fairly* straightforwardly of subatomic particles.) (2) Biological facts supervene on molecular facts; two creatures cannot be isomorphic molecule-for-molecule and not be biologically exactly alike. (3) Psychological facts supervene on biological facts; two organisms cannot have the same biological structure, be in the same total biological state in parallel environmental circumstances, *and* differ in their psychological states. (4) Supervenience is transitive. Therefore, (5) psychological facts supervene on microphysical facts of the sort that are presently (fairly) well-known. It seems to follow that physical$_2$ facts alone would suffice to determine sense-impressions at the personal level, whether or not there are sensa, and so there is no need to posit the sensa, despite the seductiveness of the "grain" argument.[36]

8. *Sensa and Microphysics*

I would now like to look briefly at the role sensa (if they exist) would play *within* microphysics.

My chief worry about sensa considered solely as microphysical objects is neither their nonparticularness nor (for the moment) their quasi-quasi-sensible properties. It is rather their strange unwillingness to venture anywhere in space save within the boundaries of sentient "core persons." This unwillingness is not strange to the psychologist, of course—he expects his posits to stay in people's heads and not wander out into the public streets. But we have seen that the psychologist is prevented by Argument G itself from doing his own positing; he has to suborn the microphysicist, just as Sellars evidently foresees. This means that the *microphysicist* will have to explain to himself why sensa occur just in the regions of space-time where they do and not throughout nature as every other microphysical object does. Evidently we are to suppose that sensa are highly specific to neural tissue. *Why would that be?* Notice that this question is far more aggravating than that of why single oxygen atoms combine stably only with pairs of hydrogen atoms, or that of why neon atoms do not combine with anything. For to say that a certain small spatiotemporal region is filled with *neural tissue* is to report a rather gross fact about molecular and hypermolecular structure. It is extremely odd at best that the possibility of a sensum's inhabiting a certain region would be dependent or conditional upon the much larger molecular environment of that region—indeed, on the whole biological system that spatially encapsulates the region. I am an enthusiastic fan of what Wimsatt (1976) calls "downward causation," but even a very powerful downward causal thrust would scarcely reach the microphysical level, which is either indeterministic or deterministic within itself.

Now, as always there is no convincing *a priori* or empirical reason to think that a being must be made of neural or even of organic matter in order to be sentient. This fact raises the question of whether Sellars would posit sensa occurring in a Martian made of silicon, or in a flawless human-stimulating android if and when such a thing should be perfected—that is, once we had determined in some responsible way that the Martian and the android were indeed sentient and had perceptual propositional attitudes more or less like ours. (Sellars seems to suggest in (1960) that he would have no serious objection to conceding this if shown the proper sort of evidence, though he cautiously refrains from taking any tough stand on the issue.) If we do choose to apply intentional perceptual descriptions to automata (as I think we shall—see the appendix), then on Sellars' principles we shall have to posit sensa occurring within them in order to account for their Manifest perceptual states. But this sharpens our original question: If our sentient android were made of metal and other "hard" materials, what would these "hard" materials have in common with neural stuff in virtue of which both would admit sensa, when sensa cannot occur within (to take Sellars' example) stone walls? It must somehow be a matter of functional organization, but this brings us directly back to the problem about downward causation.

What sort of scientific *law* would mandate the microphysically startling shyness of sensa? Not a microphysical law, so far as I can see. For Sellars, the occurrence of a neurophysiological event involving a sensum scientifically *counts as* the counterpart of a perceptual event. (It is tempting to say that a sensum's *esse* is *percipi*, but this would be wrong, since sensa are not perceived, but only scientifically underlie perceiv*ing*.) So perhaps the shyness is entailed by a biophysical law, whatever such a law might look like.

Very likely I am looking at sensa in one or more wrong ways, and in any case Sellars would be justified in putting off these questions indefinitely, pending the development of some considerably less particle-infested physics than our present one.[37] But what might some of his options be?

I have been assuming that sensa are nonparticulate companions of particles—of comparable size, for example, perhaps even sub-subatomic. But perhaps sensa are larger, and correspond not to individual subatomic particles but to systems of particles, as big as molecules or even as big as whole neurological systems. This would obviate both my earlier methodological objection to sensa and my present worry about shyness. (Indeed, Sellars has indicated to me that he does intend sensa to be "big" rather than micro-particle-sized.)

The problem I see for this suggestion is that if a sensum were to be of a larger order of magnitude than a particle, it would have spatial parts. And it seems clear that anything that has spatial parts has spatial constituents. If so, then the Principle of Reducibility applies to the sensum: any proper part of a spatial region occupied by a sensum, however small, must share that sensum's quasi-quasi-sensible property or properties. So *something* of subatomic size must have such a property, and that something therefore itself fits Sellars' definition of sensum. If this is right, it follows that there are "big" sensa only if there are little sensa in any case; and the methodological objection and the shyness problem return with their original force.[38]

A second reconstrual of sensa is suggested by Sellars' own doubts about their being particulars at all; although he tends to believe that sensa are particulars, he is not wedded to this and is willing to consider the possibility that sensa are merely "aspects" or "dimensions" of an underlying nonparticulate building material. This might make it easier to understand why sensa are not detectable by microphysics *ex officio*, and why they occur only in certain sorts of biological structures and not throughout physical space.

I am not sure what Sellars might mean by an "aspect" or a "dimension," but the most natural way of construing those expressions is to regard them as referring to *states* of the underlying building material. (The idea is, then, that the underlying stuff can simultaneously be in states of at least two different kinds: particulate-type states and sensa-type states.) Now, if a sensum is a state of an *aggregate* of the underlying entities, the Principle of Reducibility will apply again, and so, since as always the monadic sensible element of the original sense-impression will have to be carried over, each of the underlying entities will have to have a quasi-quasi- or quasi-quasi-quasi-sensible property itself, and so it would be the underlying entities that would be the ultimate sensa-particulars again. Suppose, therefore, that a sensum is a state of a single logical subject—e.g., field F is brown-sensum-ing in region R.

This seems to be a coherent notion and not to fall afoul of the Principle of Reducibility. But I do not see that it helps us much with our two difficulties. That a field is brown-sensum-ing in a certain region is not the sort of thing that microphysics would discover with any conceivable kind of apparatus; again, they would have to be doing the psychologists a favor. And they would be stuck with the shyness problem just as before, since we would still not expect hyperstructure to affect the behavior of the fields (by hypothesis, the fields would be the absolutely fundamental stuff of which the world is made).

Let me raise a third problem about the function of sensa within microscience: In what way do they *function* at all? How do they figure in the mechanics of perception? They are supposed to be required for the explanation of someone's having a perceptual propositional attitude, but the argument for this is *a priori*, and does not depend on any idea of what the sensa actually do. This by itself is no fault of Sellars'; he does not claim to have finished or even begun the actual microscience of perception. My problem is in seeing how sensa *could* function within a swarm of particles to produce perceptual propositional attitudes at the personal level. If they were *literally* colored, triangular, or whatever, we might perhaps construe the derivative quasi-redness of a red-and-triangular sensing in the Manifest Image as ultimately being a matter of the occurrence of the right red and rectangular sensa in the system of objects that is that sensings' scientific counterpart. But, as Sellars remarks in (1963b), nerves are not colored inside like chocolate candies; the characteristic properties of sensa are microproperties. The problem is exacerbated a bit by Sellars' praiseworthy insistence that sensa are not perceived by their hosts.

Sellars seems to share this worry in (1963b). In comparing sensa to Hobbes' "phantasms," he writes,

> Epiphenomenalism is a far more radical dualism than the Cartesian dualism of matter and mind. For the latter is, at least in intention, a dualism of interacting substances. Phantasms, being the counterparts of the having of sense impressions, are fleeting particulars with none of the attributes of thinghood. They neither act nor are acted on, but simply occur. (Pp. 102ff.)

Epiphenomena of this sort offend Sellars' naturalism, and properly so in my opinion. If sensa are to be posits of microscience they must be conceived of as playing some causal role in the production of human behavior.[39] But Sellars' ensuing discussion is less an attempt to defend himself against the anticipated accusation of epiphenomenalism than a series of replies to some possible misunderstandings of his position. He still owes us, I think, at least a fanciful sketch of how sensa *might* affect cognitive processes, in such a way as to demand mention in a causal explanation of behavior.

9. *Against Argument G*

We have seen that sensa are both methodologically and substantively troublesome when considered as microscientific objects, though we have not yet impugned Sellars' argument for them in any specific way. In this section I want to return to a pivotal component of Argument G and bring out a problem raised directly by it. The component I have in mind is the analogical character of the formation of our quasi-quasi-sensory microtheoretical concepts.

The quasi-quasi-color of a sensum is supposed to be analogous to the color of a Manifest physical object (the Sherwin-Williams color that seems to be smeared all over things, as George Pappas puts it). Now what, in *any* microphysics, could be analogous to a homogeneous color expanse? As Sellars himself is the first to appreciate, homogeneous color expanses seem to be *sui generis*.

Sellars often suggests that the analogy between the quasi-quasi-colors of sensa and the putatively objective colors of Manifest objects, like the analogy between the latter and the adverbial quasi-colors of sensings, is what he calls a *formal*, as opposed to a material, analogy. That is, the physical$_1$ properties of sensa taken together form a relational structure, the relations in question being things like resemblance to, difference from, and incompatibilities with each other along various parameters, and this relational structure is *isomorphic* to that similarly ordered relational structure constituted by the whole family of ostensible Manifest colors and shapes along distinct but corresponding macrophysical parameters. (Sellars remarks that this relational isomorphism is "the *essential* feature of the analogy" (1956, p. 193).) But a purely relational analogy will not do the job of establishing the inability of physical$_2$ predicates to serve as the genuine successor predicates of adverbial color- and shape-sensing terms. That is, if a purely relational analogy does suffice for Sellars' purposes of explaining theoretical concept formation, then it is hard to see why he thinks that sensa in particular are required to bear the success or properties. After all, we could appeal to a specially rigged family of numbers or sets, designed to exhibit precise relational isomorphism to our family of ordinary ostensible colors and shapes (relative to some chosen parameters or other). More to the point, it would probably be easy enough to find suitable parameters relative to which a family or ordinary physical$_2$ neurophysiological events displayed a relational isomorphism to the family of ostensible colors and shapes; and that would open the way to precisely the sort of physical$_2$ role-occupant reduction of sensings that Sellars is at great pains to combat. It seems, then, that some nonrelational, qualitative similarity between ostensible colors and the quasi-quasi-colors of sensa will be required if we are to allow Sellarsian explanations of ostensible perceivings to go through *and* to necessitate the positing of sensa.

(Perhaps Sellars actually agrees with this. In (1978) he writes,

> I have come to see . . . that we must be able so to formulate the analogy between manners of sensing and perceptual attributes of physical objects [to take the other branch of Sellars' duple analogical dependence], that it is made evident that the analogy preserves in a strict sense the conceptual *content* of predicates pertaining to the perceptual attributes of physical objects, while transposing this content into the radically different categorical framework to which manners of sensing belong. . . . [It] is necessary to explain the sense in which color concepts preserve their content throughout their migration from the [M]anifest [I]mage to the [S]cientific [I]mage.
> . . . In particular, the idea that there is a sense in which conceptual content can be preserved through a change of category seems to me necessary to give meaning to the idea that the *very pinkness and cubicity* of pink ice cubes can be *somehow* present in ostensible seeings of pink ice cubes *as* pink ice cubes. (Pp. 13–14)

I am not sure, though, what Sellars means by "conceptual content" here.)

If some nonrelational, qualitative similarity must obtain between the colors of Manifest objects and the quasi-quasi-sensible properties of sensa, what could it be? The trouble is, to put it crudely, that anything that is at all like a color in a *nonrelational*, nondispositional way is a color. It is in this sense, it seems to me, that Berkeley was right in holding colors to be *sui generis*.[40] The immediate consequence is that if there are sensa, they are not merely quasi-quasi-colored, but literally colored, and I take it that the presence of literally colored objects in microphysics, particulate or not, is something so pyrotechnically Anaxagorean that Sellars rejects it as vehemently as most people do.

A possible answer to this horn of my dilemma is that homogeneity *is* the required similarity between the color of a Manifest object and the quasi-quasi-color of a sensum; perhaps all a sensum has to do in order to serve successfully as the Scientific-Image locus of color is to have one or more of its properties homogeneously. But this answer cannot be right: For if sensa are ultimate entities or simples, in the sense of having no constituents, they satisfy the homogeneity requirement trivially. *Any* ultimate simple has *all* its properties homogeneously, even its relational properties, if the standard definition of homogeneity as homeomerousness is what Sellars has in mind:

> x is homogeneously F $=$ $_{df}$ Every (proper or improper) part of x is F.

A punctiform simple, in particular, would have all its properties homogeneously, and so no sensa would be required to exhibit the weak qualitative analogousness we are considering. Some more distinctive qualitative property is needed to do the job—more distinctive than merely a homogeneous property that occupies the appropriate niche in the logical space of colors, but less distinctive than literal, vivid, aesthetically interesting color itself. What property could that possibly be? And how could scientists ever know that they had discovered it?

This difficulty concerning homeomerousness seems to expand, in fact, into a general problem for Sellars' philosophical use of sensa: The properties of sensa are supposed to be analogous to the colors of Manifest objects in a way that at least crucially *involves* their being homogeneous. But we have seen that sensa (if there are any) have properties homogeneously in a degenerate way, and not because of the special nature of sensa or of their quasi-quasi-sensible properties themselves. Does this not simply destroy the analogy, or at least weaken it to the point of uselessness for Sellars' purposes of explaining conceptual evolution?

The difficulty also makes it a bit harder to see why Sellars insists in the first place that homogeneity is the, or even a, key feature of the analogy that supports the formation of Jones' concept of quasi-brownness and the rest. Certainly the perceived homogeneity of Manifest color and the homogeneity of quasi-color needs explanation and so must be accounted for in the Scientific Image; but does it follow that there must *be* something in the Scientific Image that has a (somehow characteristic) property homogeneously? Richardson and Muilenburg (1982) understand Sellars as simply insisting that "it is a defining characteristic of manifest objects that they are colored, and a defining characteristic of colors that they are homogeneous" (p. 32). Thus, "to purge homogeneity as part of the . . . analogy would be to make nonsense of the model and, hence, also of the analogy itself." The matter may be as simple as this, but it has a decided ring of bare assertion.

One might think of spelling out Sellars' idea of the "logical space" of a family of properties, which figures in the relational isomorphisms that constitute formal analogies, in terms of property *orders*. (This too is astutely suggested by Richardson and Muilenburg.) Two things

that are formally analogous share a single set of *second-order* properties—most visibly, the relations that obtain between their first-order
properties and relations. We might, then, simply define "formal analogy" as a sharing of second-order properties in this way. Richardson
and Muilenburg remark that homogeneity itself is a second-order
property; so perhaps Sellars' reason for insisting that homogeneity is
part of the analogy is that he understands "formal analogy" in this
way.

This will not quite do, for as I have said in section 2, it is not strictly
true to call homogeneity a second-order property. "Homogeneous" is
not a predicate applied to abstract singular terms. The property
brownness itself is not homogeneous. What is true instead is that some
(zeroth-order) things have brownness homogeneous*ly*, which is
simply to say that every part of them is brown. Again, if homogeneity
is a *property* at all, as opposed to some other kind of Fregean intension, it is a property of property instantiatings or something of the
sort. Sellars may still want to insist that properties of this slightly
more complex type be part of any formal analogy in any case; but
some defense of this demand still seems called for.

10. Possibilities for Sellarsian Color in the Scientific Image

Rather than continue to search for flaws in Argument G, I would like
to close by suggesting some alternative ways of locating color in the
Scientific Image—that is, some other possible "ultimate inheritors"
of the sensible quality dimension, that I think should have received
a bit more consideration by Sellars.

Richardson and Muilenburg suggest a possibility: Why *not* posit
little subjects of quasi-quasi-sensings in the Scientific Image (option
[c] of section 5)? These little people would not be Cartesian egos,
notice, because they would be spatial just as sensa are. I agree that
this sounds weird, but I do not see that it sounds much weirder than
sensa. Probably Sellars would reply that at least sensa allow us to
reduce sentient beings to a microphysical level of reality at which
there are no sentient beings, while Richardson and Muilenburg's suggestion would leave sentience an unexplicated surd in nature.

Alternatively, as James Cornman (1974) asked, why is Sellars so
sure that particles cannot be colored? Why would it be unreasonable
to maintain that a subatomic particle takes on a color when it interacts
with certain other particles in certain ways? Of course, particles are
too small to be seen at all, so we do not observe their chameleon-like
antics.

In a reply to Cornman, Noren (1975) reminds us of Heisenberg's methodological dictum (1937, p. 119) to the effect that it is impossible to explain the Manifest qualities of ordinary middle-sized objects "except by tracing these back to the behavior of entities which themselves no longer possess these qualities." All very well, but Heisenberg did not have the "grain" argument to contend with. Besides, his principle does not seem to be true in full generality; so far as I can see it is perfectly appropriate to explain a macro-object's having the *mass* it does by reference to the combined masses of its ultimate constituents. Besides, even if there is a principled scientific reason why it would be improper to speak of particles' being literally colored, there is no obvious reason why particles could not be *quasi-quasi-* colored, and that is all that is required by Sellars' form of argument; we need only find a Scientific counterpart, and until we have been told more about what kind of distinctive quality "quasi-quasi-color" might be, we will not be able to see why no particle could have it.[41]

Chapter 9

Freedom of the Will and the Spontaneity of Consciousness

Materialism, and Functionalism in particular, suggest a causal determinism regarding human thought and action, and such determinism occasions worries about both freedom of the will[1] and the evident spontaneity of consciousness. In this chapter I shall try to allay those worries; for they are entirely groundless.

1. The Problem of Freedom of the Will

Here is what I take to be the basic problem:

1. Every event has a determining cause. (That is, for any event e, there exists a set of antecedent causal conditions that are jointly sufficient for e's occurrence; given those conditions, e could not but have occurred.) [The thesis of Determinism]
2. A human action is at least an event (i.e., a happening or occurrence). [Trivial]
3. If an action has a determining cause, then it is not a *free* action in the sense germane to moral responsibility.

Yet 4. (Many) human actions are free in the moral sense.

Unfortunately, the foregoing is an inconsistent set; 1–4 cannot all be true. 2 I take to be innocuous and include only parenthetically. So 1, 3, or 4 must go. Yet each is initially plausible.

2. The Initial Plausibility of the Premises

Thesis 1, one version of Determinism, is firmly endorsed by common sense, in that when any interesting event occurs we automatically assume there to be a sufficient causal explanation. (Two examples: (i) One morning your toaster explodes, blasting a nasty hole in your kitchen wall. You take it to an appliance repairperson. The repairperson says, "Right, that happens sometimes; there is no cause." You say, "Oh, good old agnogenic systems failure, I suppose?" The repairperson responds, "No, I don't mean I don't know the cause—I mean I do know there simply was none." At that point you go and find a new repairperson. (ii) You wake up one morning with a livid, ugly rash all over your body. You see a dermatologist. The dermatologist says your condition is quite common. It has no cause; it just happens. As in the toaster case, the dermatologist is not confessing ignorance, but saying positively that the rash is a random, quite uncaused event. You go and find a new dermatologist.)

Some philosophers have thought that 1 is an *a priori* truth delivered by metaphysical intuition; it is closely akin to the Principle of Sufficient Reason, and can be regarded as a slight generalization of "Ex nihilo nihil fit." Science vindicates common sense in this case: For a physical event to occur uncaused would (it seems) be for matter-energy to come into the system out of nowhere, which is disallowed by the conservation laws again.

Two qualifications are needed here: (i) *At the microlevel,* determinism probably does not hold. There are quantum phenomena that seem to be genuinely indeterministic, even though some physicists insist that there are "hidden variables" or underlying mechanisms. However, these phenomena effectively cancel each other out, and at the macrolevel determinism still holds as near as matters. (ii) Suppose Cartesian Dualism is correct. Then there may be nonphysical mental events that are not determined; the mental has a way of seeming spontaneous. Let us therefore restrict the argument to physical events, since it is the physical aspects of human action that concern us primarily in moral evaluation. Thus, 1 and 2 should be qualified: "Every *physical macro*-event has a determining cause," and "A human action (of the sort that concerns us) is a physical macro-event."

Thesis 3 is supported by a consideration of when and why we exculpate. There are cases in which it is completely uncontroversial that an agent or "agent" is not to be held responsible, and what they seem to have distinctively in common is that the agent's deed has a determining cause. Clear cases include (a) insuperable physical restraint, (b) insuperable physical illness (such as coma), (c) psychiatric illness that turns its victim into an automaton, such as psychomotor epilepsy in some forms.

Many philosophers want to grant that there are other, less dramatic cases of exculpatory "unfreedom" also: criminality that is to some degree compulsive, such as kleptomania; drug addiction; Freudian compulsion; and even coercion by pistol. As against this, Jean-Paul Sartre (1946; 1956, especially part I, chapter II) has argued that *typical* cases of these latter sorts are not cases of one's literally *having no choice*. Rather, they are cases in which a deliberate choice is made between two alternatives one of which the agent prefers considerably to the other. We humans often rationalize by pretending that we "had no choice" when clearly (when you think about it) we *made* a choice (we choose to smoke, we choose to seduce or to be seduced, we choose to hand over our wallets at gunpoint). Sartre is quite right to anathematize this pretense as "bad faith."[2] Let us say that a person is "unfree" to do X in the moral sense just in case that person is unable to do X *no matter how much or how single-mindedly he wants to do X*. Of course, there are often exculpatory factors. But that is how they should be seen: not as somehow physically *preventing* the agent from doing something, but as making it overwhelmingly and uncontroversially reasonable for the agent to choose not to do that thing.[3]

Thesis 4 is supported both by common sense and by phenomenology. Surely in ordinary choice situations, we could have done otherwise. And surely, we *are* morally responsible much of the time. Otherwise, our entire moral life makes no sense, and our system of criminal justice is a cruel joke. There may be utilitarian social reasons for jailing people who commit crimes, but we ought to have qualms about this if the people genuinely *do not deserve* punishment and are morally guiltless. Also, as Campbell (1957) advises, consider the phenomenology of deliberation. When you are deciding whether to move your finger an inch to the right or an inch to the left, what could be more obvious than that the choice is up to you? If it is instead true that you are helpless in the grip of forces beyond your control, then you are under a great illusion. And if free will is an illusion, the illusion is a *grand* illusion, a corker, something that only a terrific Evil Demon could generate.

There are obviously, three positions we might take, each having a traditional name: (a) *Hard Determinism*. Keep 1 and 3, and bite the bullet, denying 4. See, e.g., Hospers (1958). (b) *Soft Determinism or "Compatibilism."* Keep 1, insist on 4, but contend contrary to 3 that 1 and 4 are compatible. (Hume, 1739, 1748; Stace, 1952; Ayer, 1954.) (c) *"Libertarianism" or "Voluntarism."* Reject Determinism. (This is Campbell's view.)

3. Soft Determinism

A strong case can be made for Soft Determinism. Here is the argument: Of our three theses, two are endorsed by common sense, and one of those two is also endorsed by science. The third, 3, has no such imprimatur; it is the most (suspiciously) *philosophical* of the three, and is defended by a relatively speculative and philosophical argument. It is tempting to insist that we *know* 1 and 4 are true; if both are true, then they are compatible, and any purely philosophical argument designed to show them incompatible must be specious.[4] Indeed, this last remark suggests a fruitful research program: Consider as many arguments for 3 as anyone can dream up, set them out as precisely as possible, and then in each case spot the purely metaphysical assumption that drives the argument; conclude that the assumption must be false. In this way we might learn much about the metaphysics of human actions and moral responsibility.

The foregoing *a priori* case is inconclusive, of course; not even common sense and science taken together are as infallible as it suggests. But it has considerable weight, and I think we would all like to be Soft Determinists if we can, i.e., if Soft Determinism is a tenable position. However, (i) the Soft Determinist has a task to perform, in that the burden is on him to come up with a clear definition of "free action" that connects appropriately and exhaustively with moral responsibility but that is also demonstrably compatible with Determinism; and (ii) there are impressive objections to Soft Determinism, pushed by Hard Determinists and Libertarians alike. Let us make an attempt at a definition of "free action," and then look at some of the objections.

The following definition is suggested by Stace and by Ayer.

I did X freely = $_{df}$
(1)   If I had wanted to (or chosen to) I would have done otherwise [this is Ayer's analysis in particular of the locution "I could have done otherwise"]; and
(2)   I did X *by choice*; X proceeded out of my own desires, beliefs, deliberation, and decision; and
(3)   I was uncoerced, uncompelled, and unconstrained.

As hordes of philosophers have pointed out, "freedom" in the moral sense contrasts with coercion or constraint, not with having a cause. The difference between free actions and actions for which I am not responsible is not that the latter are uncaused, which would make little sense, but that the two have causes of significantly different kinds—the first inner and psychological, involving my own act of will, and the second external, bypassing my desires and intentions and making them irrelevant to the outcome.

Note that our clear, uncontroversial cases of "unfreedom" do not even begin to satisfy the above definition; they violate *each* of the three conditions. (Let us continue to distinguish "exculpation" of two different sorts: Sometimes we absolve someone of blame because he was literally not responsible—he had a rock on his chest or was in a coma. In other cases we exculpate, not because the person was not responsible, but because his decision was completely reasonable and understandable, as when you hand over your Vegemite at gunpoint instead of returning it to its rightful owner. Ayer and others have garbled the issue by confusing these two sorts of exculpation.)

4. Objections and Replies

(I) Richard Taylor (1974) has asked why it should matter that my action X was caused by a choice of mine rather than by something extrinsic, *when my choice itself had a determining cause.* It was determined in advance which way I would choose, and so the action X arising out of my choice can hardly be called free after all. To see this, consider two more examples. (i) An evil scientist uses an infernal machine to cause an innocent bystander to *form the desire* to kill a third party. The desire thus artificially formed is so powerful that the bystander picks up a gun and shoots the victim. (ii) An evil and lascivious scientist invents the perfect *and subtle* aphrodisiac. Rather than acting directly upon glands and muscles (cf. note 2), the new drug acts on the brain and simply produces overwhelming desires. Taylor's moral is that if I have a machine or a drug that completely controls people's desires, beliefs, and intentions, then those people are my puppets just as surely as if I had put straitjackets on them. Even though the control is now more subtle, they are not free or responsible.

Reply:[5] This all seems right, but notice it does not prove the full general thesis 3. What we object to in these cases is precisely that the victim is the puppet of another person—that his or her *choices* are coerced. Therefore we can patch up our analysis by simply adding a fourth condition:

(4) My choice itself was uncoerced, uncompelled, and unconstrained.

This seems to do the trick. It is somewhat *ad hoc,* but I think it also does capture part of our concept of freedom.

(II) But "do not all causes equally necessitate?" Why does it matter that one kind of cause is "inner" and the other is "external" or "extrinsic"?

Reply (Ayer): It depends on what one means by "necessitate." If "necessitate" just means "to be causally sufficient for," then of course all causes equally necessitate, i.e., all causes cause. But this is trivial, tautologous, and so cannot affect the argument. However, if "necessitate" means "coerce" or "compel," the answer is *no*—the Soft Determinist position is precisely that only some kinds of causes are correctly described as "coercion" or "compulsion." Hard Determinists and Libertarians alike often pull a rhetorical trick on the Soft Determinist, viz., that of *personifying* an action's antecedent causal conditions: "The events of your early childhood *force* you to do what you're doing now; they have you helpless in their grip; you are completely in their power!" But this is all metaphor, metaphor designed to mislead us into seeing what are in fact normal inner causes as extrinsic, coercive causes.

(III) Even so, if the distinction between free actions and actions for which I am not responsible is just a difference between two kinds of causes, between causal pathways of two different shapes, why does it or should it have the enormous moral significance we attach to it? (When a causal chain bends in one way, we pat you on the head and give you a sandwich; when it bends the other way we throw you in jail.) Is this not completely irrational?

Reply: I grant that this seeming arbitrariness is troublesome. But notice that it is by no means confined to the free-will issue. Distinctions between causal pathways of different shapes pervade our moral life. A *forged check* is just a check with the wrong sort of etiology. A *counterfeit bill* is just one that came from a printing press on the wrong side of the tracks. A forged painting lacks the right provenance; etc. Yet we make sharp evaluative distinctions in each case. Maybe this is irrational; certainly it can be made to sound suspicious. But it is entirely natural and commonplace.[6]

(IV) Campbell objects specifically to Ayer's analysis of "I could have done otherwise" (clause (1)). Ayer interprets the latter locution *hypothetically*, as meaning "would have *if*." But, Campbell maintains, *real* freedom, real could-have-done-otherwise-ness, is unconditional and categorical. When I am genuinely free in choosing, I could do otherwise, period, not could have *if* something-or-other else were true. For consider: Why is it relevant what I would have done if I had had other wants from the ones I actually did have? The fact is I did have those wants, and it was antecedently determined that I would have those wants, and given those wants and the surrounding circumstances it was inevitable that I would do what I did.

Reply: Up till the phrase "For consider," these Campbellian remarks constitute just a bare *assertion* that Ayer's analysis and others like it are incorrect, not an argument to *show* that (and why) hypothetical analyses are incorrect. The argument has to be the part that comes after "For consider." But the part just restates objection (I) above, and objection (I) has already been answered.[7]

(V) Taylor argues (1974, chapter 6, and elsewhere), that if I *know in advance* what I am going to decide to do, then my "deliberation" is a sham and my resulting act is not a free one. Indeed, if I know in advance what I am going to do, then I cannot be said to *decide* or *choose* to do it, and so (even by Ayer's own analysis) it is not a free act in the moral sense. But if Determinism is true, then I can know in advance everything I am going to do (I would know all these things if I were told a complete previous state of the relevant part of the world and given the laws of nature and a pocket calculator). Therefore, if Determinism is true as the Soft Determinist claims, I am not free as the Soft Determinist claims; Soft Determinism must go.

It does not really help to point out that I *do not* ever know for sure what I am going to decide, for surely freedom in the moral sense is not just a matter of my ignorance; a clever predictor with a powerful pocket calculator could not turn me from a responsible agent into a puppet just by telling me something.

Reply: It is tempting to concede that if I do know in advance what I am going to do, then I cannot genuinely decide or choose to do it; Taylor's famous story of Osmo[8] is fairly convincing. But (i) we may just want to deny the principle on the strength of Soft Determinism's plausibility (cf. the *a priori* argument formulated above); that I know what I will do does not entail that I am in any way coerced to do it. Moreover, (ii) even if this principle is true, it does not entail that if there is *anyone*—God, or someone other than myself—who can predict what I am going to do then I am not free. That more general claim is far less obvious. For that matter, there may be a good, clear, and relevant sense in which despite the truth of Determinism I *cannot* know what I am going to do—the initial conditions may be completely inaccessible to us. (iii) If point (ii) sounds like resting freedom upon ignorance again—even though the ignorance be permanent and insuperable—recall that in any case epistemic matters have nothing to do with constraint, coercion, and compulsion. Suppose I know that circumstances are going to cause me to want to do X, to form the intention to do X, and consequently to do X. Then (trivially) it follows that I am going to want to do X, form the intention to do X, and consequently do X. It does *not* follow that I do not do X voluntarily, of my own free will, etc. If all the right conative states are in play, then all the right conative states are in play.[9]

There are other, still more subtle criticisms of Compatibilism.[10] They would have to be addressed one by one. But our divide-and-conquer strategy has been quite successful so far. And given our original *a priori* argument, I see no ground for doubting that Compatibilism will always come through.

5. *The Spontaneity of Consciousness*

Sartre (1956) claimed to see a connection between features of consciousness and freedom of the will. This alleged connection might well be written off as a "headless woman" fallacy, as a Campbellian mistaking of our phenomenological failure to detect physical causes with some authoritative perception that our actions have no physical causes. But I think it is not simply that; an argument can be made, if only in perhaps off-puttingly Sartrean terms (for the general lines of this argument I am indebted to McInerney, 1979):

1. All the objects of consciousness that are "set over against us" have meaning for us.
2. Meaning involves value, and hence also Nonbeing. [Cf. McInerney, 1979, p. 665]
3. Value presupposes ends.

So

4. All consciousness involves ends, i.e., possibly nonexistent states of affairs that are desired or aimed at.
5. No end is strictly determined by another end. [A Deweyan point; cf. McInerney (1979), pp. 666ff.]
6. What is now the case is "pure positivity" or Being. [Sartrean principle]
7. Nonbeing cannot be produced by Being. [Sartrean principle]

Thus

8. No end is produced (or determined or caused) by what is now the case.

And so

9. Consciousness, in producing ends, is entirely free.

Our wills are *radically* free, save when (Sartre admits) we run up against our "facticity," as when the airplane in which we are riding smacks at high speed into a mountain, or (I presume) when we try to strike a match on a wet cake of soap.

My quarrel would be with whatever background principle licenses the inference of 8. But I now venally leave it to the reader to adjudicate the matter.

Epilogue

Argument, even clever and inspired argument, has failed to damage Homunctionalism. Only muttering and posturing remain. Yet, on the basis of wide experience, I predict that many "qualia" enthusiasts will be stolidly unconvinced even after reading all the foregoing pages. It is a curious feature of the mind-body problem that "qualia"-oriented opponents of materialism tend to be simply unmoved by argument *and seem to feel quite justified in being so.*[1] (Tit-for-tat, materialists remain unembarrassed by the lack of any particularly convincing argument for materialism other than the general aesthetic and scientistic considerations I have sketched in chapter 1.)

I close this essay with a simple appeal: If you now find yourself thinking that there is still a "qualia"-based problem for Homunctionalism, ask yourself (sincerely and clear-headedly) the following questions:

—Are you allowing several different objections to slop over into each other, instead of focusing on a specific objection?[2]

—Are you a victim of Armstrong's (1968a) "headless woman illusion," also known as the "introspective fallacy," i.e., that of inferring that because you do not detect that a mental state has physical property *P*, you (successfully) detect that the state does not have *P*?

—Are you making facile errors about imaginability? (Cf. chapter 2; also, e.g., Hill (1981), Levine (1983))

—Are you committing any modal fallacy, as in Leibniz's Law objections and some versions of Kripke's argument?

—Are you falling victim to the Gestalt phenomenon described in chapter 5, instead of seeing the forest as well as the trees?

—Are you committing the "stereopticon" fallacy noted in chapter 7?

—Have you slipped on the Banana Peel? (This is a watchbird watching *you*.)

Here ends my catechism. If you can honestly and lucidly answer "No" to each of these questions, you are probably a clearer thinker than I, since the temptations are always there, each waiting to ensnare you while you are busy guarding against one of the others. But if despite the difficulty you *can* honestly and lucidly answer "No" throughout and you still have "qualia" symptoms, then I surmise that you must be ready to come out of the closet on phenomenal individuals, for I can think of no other possible source of the symptoms (given honesty and lucidity). In that case, my advice is: *Do it*. You have nothing to lose but the world.

Appendix: Machine Consciousness[1]

Artificial Intelligence is, very crudely, the science of getting machines to perform jobs that normally require intelligence and judgment. Researchers at any number of AI labs have designed machines that prove mathematical theorems, play chess, sort mail, guide missiles, assemble auto engines, diagnose illnesses, read stories and other written texts, and converse with people in a rudimentary way. This is, we might say, intelligent behavior.

But what is this "intelligence"? As a first pass, I suggest that intelligence of the sort I am talking about is a kind of flexibility, a responsiveness to contingencies. A dull or stupid machine must have just the right kind of raw materials presented to it in just the right way, or it is useless: the electric can opener must have an appropriately sized can fixed under its drive wheel *just so,* in order to operate at all. Humans (most of us, anyway) are not like that. We deal with the unforeseen. We take what comes and make the best of it, even though we may have had no idea what it would be. We play the ball from whatever lie we are given, and at whatever angle to the green; we read and understand texts we have never seen before; we find our way back to Chapel Hill after getting totally lost in downtown Durham (or downtown Washington, D.C., or downtown Lima, Peru).

Our pursuit of our goals is guided while in progress by our ongoing perception and handling of interim developments. Moreover, we can pursue any number of different goals at the same time, and balance them against each other. We are sensitive to contingencies, both external and internal, that have a very complex and unsystematic structure.

It is almost irresistible to speak of *information* here, even if the term were not as trendy as it is. An intelligent creature, I want to say, is an *information-sensitive* creature, one that not only *registers* information through receptors such as sense-organs but somehow stores and manages and finally uses that information. Higher animals are intelligent beings in this sense, and so are we, even though virtually nothing is known about how we organize or manage the vast, seething profusion of information that comes our way. And there is one sort of machine that is information-sensitive also: the digital computer. A computer *is* a machine specifically designed to be fed complexes of information, to store them, manage them, and produce appropriate theoretical or practical conclusions on demand. Thus, if artificial intelligence is what one is looking for, it is no accident that one looks to the computer.

Yet a computer has two limitations in common with machines of less elite and grandiose sorts, both of them already signaled in the characterization I have just given. First, a (present-day) computer must be *fed* information, and the choice of what information to feed and in what form is up to a human programmer or operator. (For that matter, a present-day computer must be plugged into an electrical outlet and have its switch turned to ON, but this is a very minor contingency given the availability of nuclear power packs.) Second, the *appropriateness* and effectiveness of a computer's output depends entirely on what the programmer or operator had in mind and goes on to make of it. A computer has intelligence in the sense I have defined, but has no judgment, since it has no goals and purposes of its own and no internal sense of appropriateness, relevance, or proportion.

For essentially these reasons—that computers are intelligent in my minimal sense, and that they are nevertheless limited in the two ways I have mentioned—AI theorists, philosophers, and intelligent laymen have inevitably compared computers to human minds, but at the same time debated both technical and philosophical questions raised by this comparison. The questions break down into three main groups or types: (A) Questions of the form "Will a computer ever be able to do X?" where X is something that intelligent humans can do. (B) Questions of the form "Given that a computer can or could do X, have we any reason to think that it does X in the same way that humans do X?" (C) Questions of the form "Given that some futuristic supercomputer were able to do $X, Y, Z, \ldots$, for some arbitrarily large range and variety of human activities, would that show that the computer had property P?" where P is some feature held to be centrally, vitally characteristic of human minds, such as thought, consciousness, feeling, sensation, emotion, creativity, or freedom of the will.

Questions of type A are empirical questions and cannot be settled without decades, perhaps centuries, of further research—compare ancient and medieval speculations on the question of whether a machine could ever fly. Questions of type B are brutely empirical too, and their answers are unavailable to AI researchers *per se*, lying squarely in the domain of cognitive psychology, a science or alleged science barely into its infancy. Questions of type C are philosophical and conceptual, and so I shall essay to answer them all at one stroke.

Let us begin by supposing that all questions of types A and B have been settled affirmatively—that one day we might be confronted by a much-improved version of Hal, the soft-spoken computer in Kubrick's *2001* (younger readers may substitute Star Wars' C3PO or whatever subsequent cinematic robot is the most lovable). Let us call this more versatile machine "Harry."[2] Harry (let us say) is humanoid in form—he is a miracle of miniaturization and has lifelike plastic skin—and he can converse intelligently on all sorts of subjects, play golf *and* the viola, write passable poetry, control his occasional nervousness pretty well, make love, prove mathematical theorems (of course), show envy when outdone, throw gin bottles at annoying children, etc., etc. We may suppose he fools people into thinking he is human. Now the question is, is Harry really a *person?* Does he have thoughts, feelings, and so on? Is he actually conscious, or is he just a mindless walking hardware store whose movements are astoundingly *like* those of a person?[3]

Plainly his acquaintances would tend from the first to see him as a person, even if they were aware of his dubious antecedents. I think it is a plain psychological fact, if nothing more, that we could not help treating him as a person, unless we resolutely made up our minds, on principle, not to give him the time of day. But how could we really tell that he is conscious?

Well, how do we really tell that any humanoid creature is conscious? How do you tell that I am conscious, and how do I tell that you are? Surely we tell, and decisively, on the basis of our standard behavioral tests for mental states, to revert to a theme of chapter 3: We know that a human being has such-and-such mental states when it behaves, to speak very generally, in the ways we take to be appropriate to organisms that are in those states. (The point is of course an epistemological one only, no metaphysical implications intended or tolerated.) We know for practical purposes that a creature has a mind when it fulfills all the right criteria. And by hypothesis, Harry fulfills all our behavioral criteria with a vengeance; moreover, he does so *in the right way* (cf. questions of type B): the processing that stands causally behind his behavior is just like ours. It follows that we are at least *prima facie* justified in believing him to be conscious.

We have not *proved* that he is conscious, of course—any more than you have proved that I am conscious. An organism's merely behaving in a certain way is no logical guarantee of sentience; from my point of view it is at least imaginable, a bare logical possibility, that my wife, my daughter, and my chairman are not conscious, even though I have excellent, overwhelming behavioral reason to think that they are. But for that matter, our "standard behavioral tests" for mental states yield practical or moral certainty only so long as the situation is not palpably extraordinary or bizarre. A human chauvinist—in this case, someone who denies that Harry has thoughts and feelings, joys and sorrows—thinks precisely that Harry is as bizarre as they come. But *what is bizarre about him?* There are quite a few chauvinist answers to this, but what they boil down to, and given our hypothesized facts all they could boil down to, are two differences between Harry and ourselves: his *origin* (a laboratory is not a proper mother), and the *chemical composition of his anatomy,* if his creator has used silicon instead of carbon, for example. To exclude him from our community for either or both of *those* reasons seems to me to be a clear case of racial or ethnic prejudice (literally) and nothing more. I see no obvious way in which either a creature's origin or its subneuroanatomical chemical composition should matter to its psychological processes or any aspect of its mentality.

My argument can be reinforced by a thought-experiment, in the spirit of chapters 3 and 5: Imagine that we take a normal human being, Henrietta, and begin gradually replacing parts of her with synthetic materials—first a few prosthetic limbs, then a few synthetic arteries, then some neural fibers, and so forth. Suppose that the surgeons who perform the successive operations (particularly the neurosurgeons) are so clever and skillful that Henrietta survives in fine style: her intelligence, personality, perceptual acuity, poetic abilities, etc., remain just as they were before. But after the replacement process has eventually gone on to completion, Henrietta will have become an artifact—at least, her body will then be nothing but a collection of artifacts. Did she lose consciousness at some point during the sequence of operations, despite her continuing to behave and respond normally? When? It is hard to imagine that there is some privileged portion of the human nervous system that is for some reason indispensable, even though kidneys, lungs, heart, and any given bit of brain could in principle be replaced by a prosthesis (for *what* reason?); and it is also hard to imagine that there is some *pro*portion of the nervous system such that removal of more than that proportion causes loss of consciousness or sentience despite perfect maintenance of all intelligent capacities.

If this quick but totally compelling defense of Harry and Henrietta's personhood is correct, then the two, and their ilk, will have not only mental lives like ours, but *moral* lives like ours, and moral rights and privileges accordingly. Just as origin and physical constitution fail to affect psychological personhood, if a creature's internal organization is sufficiently like ours, so do they fail to affect moral personhood. We do not discriminate against a person who has a wooden leg, or a mechanical kidney, or a nuclear heart regulator; no more should we deny any human or civil right to Harry or Henrietta on grounds of their origin or physical makeup, which they cannot help.

But this happy egalitarianism raises a more immediate question: *In real life,* we shall soon be faced with medium-grade machines, which have some intelligence and are not "mere" machines like refrigerators or typewriters but which fall far short of flawless human simulators like Harry. For AI researchers may well build machines that will appear to have some familiar mental capacities but not others. The most obvious example is that of a sensor or perceptron, which picks up information from its immediate environment, records it, and stores it in memory for future printout. (We already have at least crude machines of this kind. When they become versatile and sophisticated enough, it will be quite natural to say that they see or hear and that they remember.) But the possibility of "specialist" machines of this kind raises an unforeseen contingency: There is an enormous and many-dimensional range of possible beings in between our current "mere" machines and our fully developed, flawless human simulators; we have not even begun to think of all the infinitely possible variations on this theme. And once we do begin to think of these hard cases, we will be at a loss as to where to draw the "personhood" line between them. How complex, eclectic, and impressive must a machine be, and in what respects, before we award it the accolade of personhood and/or of consciousness? There is, to say the least, no clear answer to be had *a priori,* Descartes' notorious view of animals to the contrary notwithstanding.

This typical philosophical question would be no more than an amusing bonbon, were it not for the attending moral conundrum: What moral rights would an intermediate or marginally intelligent machine have? Adolescent machines of this sort will confront us much sooner than will any good human simulators, for they are easier to design and construct; more to the moral point, they will be designed mainly as *labor-saving devices,* as servants who will work for free, and servants of this kind are (literally) made to be exploited. If they are intelligent to any degree, we should have qualms in proportion.

I suggest that this moral problem, which may become a real and pressing one, is parallel to the current debate over animal rights. Luckily I have never wanted to cook and eat my Compaq Portable.

Suppose I am right about the irrelevance of biochemical constitution to psychology; and suppose I was also right about the coalescing of the notions *computation, information, intelligence*. Then our mentalized theory of computation suggests in turn a computational theory of mentality, and a computational picture of the place of human beings in the world. In fact, philosophy aside, that picture has already begun to get a grip on people's thinking—as witness the filtering down of computer jargon into contemporary casual speech—and that grip is not going to loosen. Computer science is the defining technology of our time, and in this sense the computer is the natural cultural successor to the steam engine, the clock, the spindle, and the potter's wheel.[4] Predictably, an articulate computational theory of the mind has also gained credence among professional psychologists and philosophers.[5] I have been trying to support it here and elsewhere; I shall say no more about it for now, save to note again its near-indispensability in accounting for intentionality (noted), and to address the ubiquitous question of computer creativity and freedom:

Soft Determinism or Libertarianism may be true of humans. But many people have far more rigidly deterministic intuitions about computers. Computers, after all, (let us all say it together:) "only do what they are told/programmed to do"; they have no spontaneity and no freedom of choice. But human beings choose all the time, and the ensuing states of the world often depend entirely on these choices.[6] Thus the "computer analogy" supposedly fails.

The alleged failure of course depends on what we think freedom really is. As a Soft Determinist, I think that to have freedom of choice in acting is (roughly) for one's action to proceed out of one's own desires, deliberation, will, and intention, rather than being compelled or coerced by external forces regardless of my desires or will. As before, free actions are not *uncaused* actions. My free actions are those that *I* cause, i.e., that are caused by my own mental processes rather than by something pressing on me from the outside. I have argued in chapter 9 that I am free in that my beliefs, desires, deliberations, and intentions are all functional or computational states and processes within me that do interact in characteristic ways to produce my behavior. Note now that the same response vindicates our skilled human-simulating machines from the charge of puppethood. The word "robot" is often used as a veritable synonym for "puppet," so it may seem that Harry and Henrietta are paradigm cases of *un*free mechanisms that "only do what they are programmed to do." This is a slander—for two reasons:

First, even an ordinary computer, let alone a fabulously sophisticated machine like Harry, is in a way unpredictable. You are at its mercy. You *think* you know what it is going to do; you know what it should do, what it is supposed to do, but there is no guarantee—and it may do something *awful* or at any rate something that you could not have predicted and could not figure out if you tried with both hands. This practical sort of unpredictability would be multiplied a thousandfold in the case of a machine as complex as the human brain, and it is notably characteristic of *people.*

The unpredictability has several sources. (i) Plain old physical defects, as when Harry's circuits have been damaged by trauma, stress, heat, or the like. (ii) Bugs in one or more of his programs. (I have heard that once upon a time, somewhere, a program was written that had not a single bug in it, but this is probably an urban folk tale.) (iii) Randomizers, quantum-driven or otherwise; elements of Harry's behavior may be *genuinely,* physically random. (iv) Learning and analogy mechanisms; if Harry is equipped with these, as he inevitably would be, then his behavior-patterns will be modified in response to his experiential input from the world, which would be neither controlled nor even observed by us. *We don't know where he's been.* (v) The relativity of reliability to goal-description. This last needs a bit of explanation.

People often say things like, "A computer just crunches binary numbers; provided it isn't broken, it just chugs on mindlessly through whatever flipflop settings are predetermined by its electronic makeup." But such remarks ignore the multileveled character of real computer programming. At any given time, as we have noted in chapter 4, a computer is running *each of any number of* programs, depending on how it is described and on the level of functional organization that interests us. True, it is always crunching binary numbers, but in crunching them it is also doing any number of more esoteric things. And (more to the point) what counts as a mindless, algorithmic procedure at a very low level of organization may constitute, at a higher level, a hazardous do-or-die heuristic that might either succeed brilliantly or (more likely) fail and leave its objective unfulfilled.

As a second defense, remember that Harry too has beliefs, desires, and intentions (provided my original argument is sound). If this is so, then his behavior normally proceeds out of his own mental processes rather than being externally compelled; and so he satisfies the definition of freedom-of-action formulated above. In most cases it will be appropriate to say that Harry could have done other than what he did do (but in fact chose after some ratiocination to do what he did, instead). Harry acts in the same sense as that in which we act, though one might continue to quarrel over what sense that is.

Probably the most popular remaining reason for doubt about machine consciousness has to do with the raw qualitative character of experience. Could a mere bloodless runner-of-programs have states that *feel to it* in any of the various dramatic ways in which our mental states feel to us?

The latter question is usually asked rhetorically, expecting a resounding answer "NO!!" But I do not hear it rhetorically, for I do not see why the negative answer is supposed to be at all obvious, even for machines as opposed to biologic humans. Of course there is an incongruity *from our human point of view* between human feeling and printed circuitry or silicon pathways; that is to be expected, since we are considering those high-tech items from an external, third-person perspective and at the same time comparing them to our own first-person feels. But argumentatively, that *Gestalt* phenomenon counts for no more in the present case than it did in that of human consciousness, viz., for nothing, especially if my original argument about Harry was successful in showing that biochemical constitution is irrelevant to psychology. What matters to mentality is not the stuff of which one is made, but the complex way in which that stuff is organized.[7] If after years of close friendship we were to open Harry up and find that he is stuffed with microelectronic gadgets instead of protoplasm, we would be taken aback—no question. But our *Gestalt* clash on the occasion would do nothing *at all* to show that Harry does not have his own rich inner qualitative life. If an objector wants to insist that computation alone cannot provide consciousness with its qualitative character, the objector will have to take the initiative and come up with a further, substantive argument to show why not.[8] We have already seen that such arguments have failed wretchedly for the case of humans; I see no reason to suspect that they would work any better for the case of robots. We must await further developments. But at the present stage of inquiry I see no compelling feel-based objection to the hypothesis of machine consciousness.

Notes

Chapter 1

1. A few pages earlier, Eddington has virtually reincarnated Descartes and (not accidentally) Russell: ". . . the mental activity of the part of the world constituting ourselves occasions no surprise; it is known to us by direct self-knowledge, and we do not explain it away as something other than we know it to be—or rather, it knows itself to be. It is the physical aspects of the world that we have to explain" (p. 267).

2. E.g., Carnap (1932/33). Note that this move sullied a vital element of positivism: the purity and diaphanousness of observation, which arose from the *immediacy* of our (alleged) acquaintance with sense-data. Assuming there are or were any, sense-data are directly perceived, in an absolute and very clear sense, without the influence of scientific theory or any other cognition. There is no such sense in which an ammeter or a bird's egg or a human conversational episode is "directly" perceived.

3. Descartes himself was well aware of the interaction problem, and corresponded uncomfortably with Princess Elizabeth on the matter. (The Princess handily got the better of him; see the exchange reprinted in Anscombe and Geach, 1954, pp. 274–286.) At one point he observed that *gravity* is causal despite its not being a klunky, kickable physical object; mysterious or not, events are brought about by gravity even though (as we now know) gravity is not even a force. The trouble with this ingenious comparison is that gravity, however understood, is at least a spatial phenomenon—gravitational fields are neatly describable in terms of the physics of space-time, while Cartesian egos are precisely not in physical space at all.

4. But see my discussion of Wilfrid Sellars' view of sensory objects, in chapter 8.

5. The Dualist has the option of maintaining that behavior is *overdetermined*, resulting from both of two perhaps parallel causal pathways, one physical and one irreducibly mental. But (a) what reason have we to believe in the latter pathway? (b) Why ever would the world be so constituted that physical-mental pairs of pathways would thus coincide? And (c) how is the alleged dual causality reflected in the relevant counterfactuals on both sides (a standard problem for epiphenomenalism)?

6. The old joke about two Behaviorists meeting on the street: The first says, "You're fine; how am I?" Ziff (1957/58) argues that the joke is misconceived, since we do not ordinarily find out how we ourselves are behaving, and we do come to know how others are feeling simultaneously with perceiving their behavior. But the point can be made in terms of inferential and non-inferential knowledge.

   If there are a "first-person" and a "third-person" perspective, might there be a *second*-person perspective that differs from both?

7. Robert van Gulick reminds me that some methodological behaviorists, including B.

F. Skinner himself, have granted that there is such a thing as introspection and that it reveals inner episodes; they deny only that the episodes thus revealed are in any way mental. (For a direct exchange on related points between Skinner and a Functionalist, see Lycan, 1984b, and Skinner 1984, p. 659). But Analytical Behaviorists and Reductive Behaviorists in philosophy have taken a more strongly negative line.

8. Kate Elgin has made the interesting point that from the standpoint of naturalism or physics-worship of the sort that motivates materialism, *counterfactual truths* are virtually as weird as mentalistic ones. All the positivists' reductive analyses of things contained scads and scads of unexplicated counterfacturals, and it was not until 1946 that Chisholm (1946) and Goodman (1947) were both struck by the intractability of subjunctives generally. They were worried in particular about the *verifiability* of counterfactuals, naturally (as well they might be), but the scientistic, naturalistic problem is there too: What is there firmly lodged in the closed causal order we call Nature that *makes* a counterfactual true, ontologically speaking? The subsequent history of the ontological problem of counterfactuals (as opposed to the semantical problem or the pragmatic problem) is littered with bleeding bodies. If we bypass early accounts that appeal to laws of nature and adopt a powerful Stalnaker/Lewisian account based on alternative possible worlds, the Behaviorist ends up saying that what it is for you to be having a visual experience of yellow is for some other person in an alternative universe actually to be asked what color the ceiling is and actually to answer "Yellow," or whatever. I think I would rather believe in Cartesian egos. (On the other hand, for a related but splendidly ingenious account, see Kraut, 1982, to be discussed and defended in chapter 8, as well as Lycan and Shapiro, 1987.)

9. A few philosophers in the positivistic and Wittgensteinian traditions have tried to argue independently against the possibility of inverted spectrum, denying that this apparent possibility is real; for a defense against these arguments, see Lycan (1973). Note, incidentally, that a Behaviorist might allow for intra*subjective spectrum inversion over time, since such an inversion gives rise to reports; I think it is peculiar to grant that possibility but also to deny the intelligibility of intersubjective inversion.

10. For other counterexamples of this type, see Bradley (1964), Campbell (1970), Kirk (1974b) and Stich (1981); for a much more sophisticated counterexample and a comparison on this score of Behaviorism with Functionalism, see Block (1981a). We shall return to this sort of issue in chapter 3.

11. Parallel points may be made against methodological behaviorism in psychology (Dennett, 1978c; Fodor, 1975; Lycan, 1984c). However, note that the present argument does not touch Eliminative Behaviorism and may even be taken to support it.

   Bob van Gulick has protested to me that Ryle himself, whom I understand as defending a version of Analytical Behaviorism, did not claim to explicate mental concepts in terms of their relations to impingements and behavior alone, but took a more holistic view of the mental concepts as a family. There is room for much fruitful disagreement here, but I cannot pause for Rylean exegesis.

12. In this book I shall reserve the term "the Identity Theory" to refer to Smart's *type-type* identification of the mental with the neurophysiological. For some Identity Theorists, a main motivation has been to explain supposed type-type correlations discovered by laboratory experiment (cf. Kim, 1966), though Smart has protested to me in correspondence that he did not share this motivation and did not mean to insist on as broad a type-type identification as that which Putnam attacked.

13. Many philosophers have the impression that Smart merely introduced a dummy term, and are unaware that there really are c-fibers that are involved in sensation.

Unfortunately (as I dimly understand the technicalities), what figure specifically in pain are not in fact c-fibers, but a-fibers.

Incidentally, there are a number of other attractive routes to the Identity Theory: (i) its avoiding of objections to *both* Dualism and Behaviorism; (ii) its explaining type-type correlations (again Smart, 1959); (iii) Armstrong's (1968b) reconception of dispositions by identifying them with their categorial bases; and (iv) the role-occupant argument of Armstrong (1968b) and Lewis (1966) taken very seriously. (However, no one seems to have noticed that this last begs the question against a two-pathway Dualism by assuming uniqueness of causes of behavior.)

Chapter 2

1. Reported and addressed by Smart (1959, footnote 13).
2. Cf. Putnam (1969) and Armstrong (1972).
3. Eric Bush (1974) interprets Richard Rorty as noting this. The allusion is to Rorty (1965).
4. Suppose someone insists to us that "Pigs have wings" entails "It snows every day in Chapel Hill." There is no way for us to *refute* this; we simply have no reason to believe it unless its proponent should come up with some unexpectedly ingenious argument. (I will argue in Chapter 9 that the "free will" issue should be reconstructed along these lines: though we cannot refute the claim that determinism is incompatible with freedom in the morally relevant sense, we have no reason to believe it either.)
5. This point is nicely elaborated by Rosenthal (1976). In my view Rosenthal's paper lays the issue peacefully to rest.
6. This formulation is essentially the same as that presented in Lycan (1974a), but the critical discussion I shall offer below is significantly altered.
7. But see Roberts (1985).
8. A similar point is made by Feldman (1974).
9. This was pointed out to me by Kripke, in his response to my (1974a) during the American Philosophical Association symposium at which it was delivered.
10. On the "KK" thesis, see Lycan (1982).
11. I thank Bob Hambourger and Michael Lockwood for discussion on this point.
12. Other distinct but also penetrating diagnoses of Kripke's problem are given by Sher (1977), Leplin (1979), Levin (1979), Hill (1981), McGinn (1981), Levine (1983), Levin (1985), and McMullen (1985).
13. On the difference, unimportant here, see Lycan (1985).
14. Perhaps not coincidentally, he has since published a book (1982) on Wittgenstein's "private language" argument, surprisingly supporting a version of the argument but with an equally surprising anti-Functionalist twist. On the latter, I have strong views, but they will have to wait.
15. As such, it was first called to my attention by Andrew Vishner, so properly it should be named "Vishner's Banana Peel."
16. Except briefly in the next four notes, in the interest of scholarship.
17. Since Smart bases one of his central arguments on the empirical discovery of type-type correlations between mental items and neurophysiological items, we have some reason to consider him a Type-Identity Theorist, and to suppose that his topic-neutral "translations" are intended to fix only the reference of mental terms. It is true that, due to pressure from Black and from Bradley (1969), Smart hesitantly adumbrates a claim to *meaning*-equivalence, but (a) he *dis*claims this at several points and continues to waffle on the point for some years, and (b) he is tempted

to claim meaning equivalence, I think, *only* because of the pressure of Black's objection, and had he been aware that no synonymy claim was needed to solve the TNP, he would gratefully have withdrawn it. Besides, unlike Armstrong and Lewis, Smart never appeals to the alleged meaning claim in any direct argument *for* his view. So we may construe Smart as maintaining that (e.g.) what is essential to *pain* is that it is the firing of c-fibers, and so on. Mental states' similarities to what is going on in their owners when . . . is *not* essential to them, but is only alluded to as a way of telling us what states Smart is talking about.

18. Armstrong never declares himself on the Type-Type issue. (I am grateful to Steve Nuttall for pointing out in detail that my earlier (1974b) branding of Armstrong as a Type-Identity theorist was entirely unjustified by the text.) We *could* construe him in exactly the way in which we just construed Smart—as using his "causal analyses" to fix the references of mental terms and then appealing to empirical science to pinpoint the terms' referents exactly and therein display the real essences of the mental entities in question. As I said in Lycan (1974a), the fact that Armstrong defends his analysis *as an analysis* goes against this interpretation; on the other hand, Armstrong waffles a bit on the meaning-preservingness of his "analyses" (p. 85), and he too, at the time he wrote, had no inkling that a solution to the TNP does not require a meaning claim. On the other hand, if confronted with the Type-Type theory's chauvinist implications, Armstrong would presumably join Lewis and the other liberals. And as I said, he is quite serious about his "causal analyses" as analyses.

19. Lewis does declare himself, rather vocally, on the Type-Type issue. Further, he does not waffle as Armstrong did on the question of whether *his* program of topic-neutral translations is supposed to be a meaning analysis. Therefore, Lewis has marked himself indelibly as a relationalist also, and thus must face the same two standard objections: his ability to accommodate inverted spectrum will depend on how careful he is in choosing his platitudes, and he too must face counterexamples of the "absent qualia" sort.

20. Smart proposed his program for "topic-neutral translations" with three main purposes in mind: (i) to answer "Black's objection"; (ii) to solve the "topic-neutrality problem" (cf. Armstrong, 1968b, pp. 76–79), which may come to the same thing; and (iii) to hinder criticisms based on Leibniz's Law.

Smart points out that there are three different kinds of properties, which we may distinguish as follows:

P   is a *physical* (or "brutely physical") property = Something's having P entails that thing's being a physical thing.

P   is a *mentalistic* (or "antiphysical") property = Something's having P entails that thing's being a mentalistic, (i.e., irreducibly nonphysical) thing.

P   is a *topic-neutral* property = P is neither a physical nor a mentalistic property. (That is, something's having P entails neither that thing's being a physical thing nor that thing's being a mentalistic thing.)

Now, take any mental ascription. (Let a "mental ascription" be a sentence that predicates some mental state of its subject.) Now, to give a *topic-neutral translation* of our mental ascription *A* is to produce a second, distinct sentence *S* that is (roughly) synonymous with *A* and that ascribes to its subject a state that it identifies only in terms of topic-neutral properties.

Smart maintains that every mental ascription *has* a correct topic-neutral translation in the foregoing sense or something like it. And this, he believes, allows him to refute the charge that any of the ascribed mental states has a property that is "nonphysical" in any damaging sense.

Moral: "Black's objection" proves that a "contingent identity" between sensations and brain processes requires that sensations have some topic-neutral properties. (Again, this is no surprise, since everything in the world has some topic-neutral properties.) Moreover, the objection proves that the *identifying* properties of sensations *qua* sensations must be topic-neutral properties if the alleged identity is to be contingently true and/or empirically known. Note: So far the topic-neutral properties that have been put forward as being the identifying properties of sensations are *relational* properties (relations between our inner state and a past stimulus). So, even though Smart is not overtly a relationalist, his view requires that sensations be identified by reference to relational properties that they have.

Chapter 3

1. Block does score a nice rhetorical point against Putnam by noting that Putnam himself (1967) made a poor effort to avoid having to admit the group consciousness of a corps of busy program-realizers; it consisted simply of stipulating that an organism may not be counted as having conscious states if that organism is decomposable into smaller organisms each of which itself realizes a similar program. This move was purely *ad hoc*, of course, and it further seems to me that the stipulated condition might well be empirically unreasonable.
2. For a fine and instructive sketch of the functional complexities of pain, see Dennett (1978c), based on Melzack and Wall (1970).
3. Block anticipates my appeal to "a developed psychology" on p. 307:

    . . . nothing we know about the psychological processes underlying our conscious mental life has anything to do with qualia. What passes for the psychology of sensation or pain, for example, is either (a) physiology, (b) psychophysics, . . . or (c) a grab-bag of descriptive studies. . . . Of these, only psychophysics could be construed as being about qualia per se. And it is obvious that psychophysics touches only the *functional* aspect of sensation, and not its qualitative character. Psychophysical experiments done on you would have the same results if done on any system Psychofunctionally equivalent to you, even if it had inverted or absent qualia. If experimental results would be unchanged whether or not the experimental subjects had inverted or absent qualia, they can hardly be expected to cast light on the nature of qualia.

    Indeed, on the basis of the kind of conceptual apparatus now available in psychology, I do not see how psychology in anything like its present incarnation *could* explain qualia.

    But even this defense of Block's intuitions begs the question, it seems. For if someone (viz., the MFist) is saying precisely that mental states, along with whatever qualitative characters they may have, are functional in nature, then that person will justifiably balk at Block's phrase "only the *functional* aspect of sensation, and not its qualitative character." Of course, here as elsewhere, Block has begged the question in a clinical sense only if the Functionalist has antecedently defended his version of Functionalism; the quality of various Functionalists' defenses of their theories is another matter.
4. A number of philosophers have held that this epistemic truism is a conceptually necessary truth. On which claim, see Lycan (1971).
5. For example, a referee for Lycan (1979a) (for whose acute comments I am grateful)

has suggested that *O* realizes S_I, *parasitically* and that the MFist may simply require that to be in *M* an organism must realize the relevant functional state *non*parasitically, in the sense that the organism must not have any proper part that is also realizing that functional state. This suggestion is natural, but admits of fairly straightforward counterexamples. To avoid these, we might refine the notion of "parasiticness" in one way or another; this would lead to a further search for counterexamples, and so it goes. But a few more promising options will be mentioned below.

6. Though Elugardo makes a well-taken historical point about Putnam.

7. Lawrence Davis (1982) suggests a similarly nonspecific tightening, alluding to ". . . 'inputs' and 'outputs' *of the right sort*. Functionalists as such have not been concerned with specifying what these right sorts may be. . . . The relevance of external physiology—or physiognomy, 'form of life', evolutionary history, or whatever— may be for others to decide" (pp. 232–233; italics original). I wonder what others Davis has in mind.

8. Alternatives to my teleological approach have been suggested. "Characteristic" inputs are picked out ultimately by social convention, as part of our "form of life" or whatever; or they are picked out by virtue of being those events that call to us most pressingly for explanation. (The former was proposed by Paul Judd in correspondence, the latter by Stephen White in conversation; I am indebted to them and to Ned Block, Brian Smith, Louis Loeb, Robert Kraut, and to the philosophy colloquium of the University of North Carolina at Greensboro for fruitful discussion of the NLA.)

   The two attempts just mentioned seem to me to have the unappetiziing consequence that whether I have a toothache depends on social convention and/or on my friends' explanatory interests. At the very least they introduce difficulties and raise awkward substantive questions that would better have been let lie. In short, the rejection of our nice, unrestricted notion of realization opens Pandora's Box. And that is the moral of the NLA.

9. In discussion of a presentation of Lycan (1981a) to the Australasian Association of Philosophy in Canberra in 1978.

10. I owe this point to Lee Bowie, in his excellent oral comments on a presentation of Lycan (1981a) at the University of Massachusetts.

11. And of course the water is "realizing" the program in the original bare sense of there existing a one-one correspondence between the discrete (possible) physical "inputs," physical states, and physical "outputs" of the water and the abstract input-letters, logical-state symbols, and output-letters, respectively, appearing in the program. But as we have seen, this mathematical notion of "realization" is useless to the Functionalist because such "realization" is too easy to achieve.

Chapter 4

1. I believe just as firmly in some form of act-utilitarianism in ethics, but the sacred principle of utility itself forbids my even telling you this, much less committing (detectable) murders in its name.

2. This multileveled hierarchical structure was noted and eloquently presented by Herbert A. Simon (1969); I do not know if the idea predates him. William C. Wimsatt has also written brilliantly on it (1976).

   Its application to psychology was first brought to my attention by Fodor (1968a) and Dennett (1975); see further references below.

3. I have in mind Lewis Thomas' (1974) discussion of insect societies and of the rela-

tion between human beings and their own mitochondria. The mereology of "organisms" is highly interest-relative. Note well, we must grant a pluralism of different reductive relations between levels of nature; consider also the entirely tenable notion of the corporation as person (Biro, 1981; French, 1984; Brooks, 1986).

4. For a rich exposition and defense of the strategy, see Cummins (1983). However, Richardson (1983) throws some fairly cold water.

5. For philosophically relevant discussion and references, see P. M. Churchland (1985b) and P. S. Churchland (1986).

6. Dennett's main concern in the work containing the following passage is the explication of intentionality. That concern is not mine here; I am interested only in homuncular breakdown *per se*.

7. In fact, as David Armstrong has pointed out to me, the present maneuver blocks a number of typical infinite-regress arguments in the philosophy of mind, including Ryle's complaint against volitional theories of deciding. Dennett himself wields it against "Hume's problem" regarding self-understanding representations (1978a, pp. 122ff.).

8. For an actual hands-on homuncular breakdown of the speech center, see figure 1, p. 262 of Lycan (1984a).

9. For stout insistence on this, see Davidson (1970).

10. Thus, Smart's example of the logic of "nation" statements' being different from the logic of "citizen" statements may have been more apropos than he imagined.

11. Popper (1972); Wimsatt (1972); Wright (1973); Millikan (1984); Neander (1981, 1983). Neander's evolutionary explication is the best I know. It is criticized with effect by E. Prior in an unpublished note and by Pargetter and Bigelow (1986); the truth seems to me to lie somewhere in between.

    Jonathan Bennett (1976) offers a different naturalistic approach to teleology due to Ann Wilbur Mackenzie (1978) (and in discussion has urged me to switch).

12. Characterizations of the contents of our space-time slice may thus be arranged in a continuum, from the least teleological to the most (highly) teleological. This continuum corresponds fairly neatly to the hierarchy of functional instantiation or realization. The molecules jointly realize, or play the role of, the piece of metal; the piece of metal plays the role of the key; the key serves as our door-unlocker; and so on. The prevalence of functional hierarchies of this kind, I believe, is what encourages ontological reduction and the idea that "everything is ultimately a matter of physics." On the relations between teleology viewed from an evolutionary perspective, functional hierarchies, ontology, and the methodology of scientific reduction, see again Wimsatt (1976). I have also profited from reading Mellick (1973), and see Matthen and Levy (1984).

13. As Jerry Fodor has pointed out to me in discussion, there is one tolerably clear distinction that a Two-Leveler might have in mind and that is absolute: it is the distinction between objects whose proper parts are essential to them and objects whose parts are not. For example, a bicycle's or even a tree's parts are replaceable, while a water molecule's parts perhaps are not (one might argue either that if the molecule were to lose one of its hydrogen or oxygan atoms it would not be *that* molecule or that without the right sorts of atoms it would not be a water molecule at all). I agree that this distinction is genuine, and I expect it has some metaphysical importance. But it has no *psychological* importance. The level of chemistry is far too low in the institutional hierarchy to affect mentation; that is, if two neuroanatomies are just the same even though they are realized by different chemicals, psychology is the same.

14. Amelie Rorty has suggested to me the Aristotelian idea of explaining an organism's

component functions (more exactly, of explaining its-functions'-constituting-its-thriving) by reference to the suitability of those functions for the material conditions of the organism's species. This idea fits well with the etiological account of function that I tend to favor. Given a relatively undifferentiated mass of "lower" biological material at a much earlier evolutionary stage, how would it clump together and articulate itself in order to face the world at large in a more robust and less vulnerable way? Its own "structural" or "material" nature would enforce some answers and suggest still others, and given selection pressures of various now retrodictable sorts it is no surprise that many or most of these answers have been realized. If "function" is understood in evolutionary terms, then, function itself gets explained in this way, in terms of the propensities of the organism's material substratum. I take that explanation to complement, rather than to compete with, "downward-causation" explanations based in higher levels of nature (of the sort Wimsatt talks about). In fact, we get a sort of pincer movement: selection pressure from much higher levels interacting with bottom-up pressure from the nature and propensities of the particular chemical constitution of the pre-existing neighborhood, the two pressures jointly molding what lies between. But one might want to emphasize the bottom-up pressure at the expense of higher-level explanations. *In some sense* that emphasis has to be right, given supervenience of top on bottom, though it is tricky to work out all the different up-down interrelations there are.

Rorty points out (in correspondence) that full-scale multiple realizability must be distinguished from mere functional characterization of states of organisms, since detailed accounts of function tend to put strict requirements on realizing-stuff; there is a trade-off here. But I do not see that the Aristotelian bottom-up explanatory strategy *per se* counts against multiple realizability. For the same functional answers or solutions might well be hit upon by chemically quite different bunches of primordial stuff. Rorty offers the example of *eating:* Computers do not eat, in any literal sense, and the earth does not ingest rain; multiple realizability fails even though the activity is functionally characterized. I want to make the same sort of rejoinder that I shall be making to an argument of Block in the next chapter: Of course computers and other (even biologic) entities do not eat; but there is an intermediate, more abstract characterization of eating itself—*holotropism* as it was called in my college biology classes—which excludes computers but includes lots of species biochemically quite different from ours; it has something to do with acquiring proteins very similar to one's own and physically homogenizing them and ingesting them and making them part of one without major rearrangement of amino acids or something of the sort—at any rate, it is a form of nourishment that is sharply distinguished from many other species' and is rather distinctive of our phylum or whatever. This point checks nicely with my usual idea of functional characterizations that hold for intermediate levels of nature and are neither too vague and general nor too chauvinistically species-bound.

15. Elliott Sober (1985) praises this attitude as "putting the function back into functionalism"; cf. my remarks on p. 27 of Lycan (1981a), regarding Putnam and Fodor's pun on the word "function."

16. For details, see Lycan (1981c).

17. Why does pain hurt? Why could we not have a damage-signaling and repair-instigating system that was not uncomfortable? The answer is simple. Suppose I had just such a system, like the red warning light on my auto engine. Just as I habitually though irrationally ignore the warning light and vaguely hope it will go away, I would ignore a personal warning light if it did not intrinsically provide me with an urgent motive to do something about it.

18. Robert van Gulick has presented me (in correspondence) with some meteorological and geological cases in which (apparent) degrees of teleologicalness do not follow levels of nature. Such cases are very much to the point, but I shall have to postpone going into them.

19. Ned Block, who violently disagrees with me on the present issues, once said (in conversation), "I'll give you *neurons* and *cells* and so on as functional, but when you come to *hydrogen* and *oxygen*, when you get right down to the level of *chemistry*, there's just nothing functional or teleological at all!!" Oh, no? "Hydro-"*what*? "Oxy-"*what??* (The shot is a cheap one but immensely satisfying.)

20. Fodor and Block (1971), Lewis (1971), Haugeland (1981), and others.

21. I owe this observation to Stan Munsat, and I am grateful both to Munsat and to Jay Rosenberg for their generous and very useful advice on the details of this section.

22. Actually there are various borderline, derivative, and hybrid cases here. *Several* distinctions actually cut across each other: alterable-only-by-snipping-and-resoldering versus alterable-in-some-other-way; alterable-from-the-keyboard versus not-so-alterable; transportable versus nontransportable; volatile versus nonvolatile (a question of whether a program persists through system resets and shutdowns); and doubtless more—even the second of these is evanescent. Whatever: Any of these notions of "software" is a considerably narrower contrasting concept to "hardware" than is "program." The same program can be marketed in any number of different forms. (The IBM PC takes LOTUS 1-2-3 from a disk; the PC Jr.'s LOTUS 1-2-3 is sold as a ROM pack; the Hewlett-Packard Notebook Portable has LOTUS 1-2-3 in ROM. For all I know there is yet another portable that has LOTUS 1-2-3 simply hardwired in my original soldering-iron sense.)

23. Michael Smith has pointed out to me in correspondence that the foregoing remarks ignore the operating system perspective. If a computer can ever be said to be running *a* single program, that program is in UNIX or the like; from this point of view, the vertical hierarchy I have sketched "is but one of many housekeeping tasks it must juggle at once, including I/O, memory management, and, for UNIX, the intricacies of time-sharing."

24. It was once made to me by, I believe, Bill Bechtel.

Chapter 5

1. Davis (1974) has made a similar point, in more detail. Both Davis' discussion and the foregoing counterintuition reinforce the positive epistemological argument I made in section 1 of chapter 3.

    I once received a letter from Ned Block, dated January 28, 1985, and sent from CSLI in Stanford. It warned me that it (the letter itself) had been saturated in a locally produced slow-acting derivative of the Jakob-Kreutzfeld virus, and that in ten years (only eight, now) I will have no qualia. "And to top it off, you won't even know it, since the virus smashes your qualia while leaving your propositional attitudes just as they are."

2. Notice the absurdity of saying, "If we were to scoop the neurons out of your head and then stuff the empty brainpan with nothing but neurons arranged in the same way, you would cease to have phenomenal experience."

3. Gregory Sheridan has reminded me that the latter is at least logically a stronger thesis, since there can be neurophysiological differences that do not constitute psychofunctional differences. So it is *eo ipso* less plausible. But I maintain it is still *very* plausible.

I am grateful to Sheridan for lengthy and penetrating correspondence on this topic.

4. Michael DePaul has pointed out a difference between a homunculi-head and a normal human being that might be relevant: if the homunculi are really little people working in more or less the same way as do the Chinese workers in Block's other example, they cannot work nearly so *rapidly* as the standard neural realization of the human program. So both the homunculi-head and the population of China would respond only very slowly to stimuli. This drastic slowing of their computational activity, though it seemingly would not affect relatively nonfeely cognitive processes, might somehow affect phenomenal experience. But this would need to be shown.

5. In (1978a, chapter 9) Dennett makes an attempt at explicating consciousness in precisely these terms; he analyzes the notion of conscious awareness in terms of inclinations to say things, and identifies such inclination with inputs to the "printout component," via the "*Control* component," from the short-term or buffer memory that holds the content of our present experience. This Rylean account has some plausibility, though I think doubt is shed on the letter of its sufficiency by the well-known "blindsight" phenomenon, in which subjects whose visual fields have been truncated as a result of brain surgery and who report a total lack of visual experience on one side nevertheless pick up considerable information about the colors and shapes of objects facing them on that side. (See Poppel, Held, and Frost, 1973, and Weiskrantz et al., 1974.)

What bothers me more about Dennett's account is that it deals only with awareness *qua* propositional attitude, and does not even address the kind of difficulty that I think Block is trying to bring out. The feel of pain, the sweetness of a taste, and the grainlessness of phenomenal color are not, or at least not *prima facie*, propositional at all.

As I shall keep on saying, it is important to distinguish a number of quite separate concerns that recent philosophers have expressed in qualia-based objections to materialist theories of the mental; materialists quite frequently and mistakenly think that in speaking to just one or the other of these concerns they have solved or dissolved the problem of qualia in its entirety. I shall catalogue them at the beginning of chapter 8.

6. "Wait till next year!" John Searle jeers in a different but very similar connection (1980). *Of course* wait till next year!

7. For some criticisms of Fodor's argument, see Dennett (1978a, chapter 6). Such criticisms are decisively rebutted in Lycan (1981c).

8. Save perhaps the "analytical functionalist," whose view I reject (see note 14).

9. Putnam (1975), Fodor (1978), Stich (1978), Burge (1979), Lycan (1981c), . . .

10. This idea is anticipated in part by Dretske (1981). See also van Gulick (1980, 1982).

11. I would also observe that some current disputes within the cognitive science community are misconceived in the Two-Levelist way. For example, the "bottom-uppers" versus the "High-Church Computationalists" (see P.S. Churchland, 1986, and Dennett, forthcoming) and the New Connectionists versus the same (see Bechtel, 1985). The New Connectionists in particular are a superb example of a bio-computational middle way. Somewhat in the same spirit is P.M. Churchland's (1986) "phase-space sandwich" model of sensorimotor coordination, based on Pellionisz and Llinas (1979, 1982); or rather, though *he* does not always think it in a mediating way, I count it as another feasible middle way *within the spirit of a properly teleologized functionalism.*

12. Wilfrid Sellars does. But that is another story, to be told in chapter 8.

13. Block does not himself stress the relational/monadic contrast, but offers his differential intuitions raw; so he may remain unmoved by my foregoing *ad hominem* and simply insist that having a neurochemistry roughly like ours is a necessary condition for experiencing qualia, relational or not. Yet, I wonder, how could a *philosopher* know *that*? Is it aglow with the Natural Light?

14. I am indebted to Sydney Shoemaker for useful correspondence on this point. For my own part, I cannot accept analytical functionalism, for two reasons: (i) I reject the alternatively conceptual-analysis or implicit-definition theory of meaning on which that theory rests. (See Armstrong, 1968b, and Lewis, 1972, for its two most explicit versions and defenses, and Lycan, 1981c, especially footnote 10, for my alternative view of the semantics of mental terms; also, for a similar view, see Jacoby, 1985.) (ii) I doubt that common sense or "folk psychology" contains enough information about mental entities to characterize their natures as richly as would be needed to avoid counterexample. Clothespin models of folk psychology would be pretty easy to come by, without the massive complexity and teleological organization that would warrant an ascription of real mentality.

15. The term is due to Dennett (forthcoming-a).

16. Here I follow some recent writers in supposing that there are really any High Church computationalists; I am not sure that any actual Functionalist has ever self-consciously intended the view. It is usually ascribed to Zenon Pylyshyn and Jerry Fodor, on the basis of some of their remarks about multiple realizability. Perhaps Ned Block does really hold it, or he would not continue to resist my case against Two-Levelism as begun in my (1981a).

17. See particularly (again) Bechtel (1985), and the references made therein.

18. Block hints on p. 309 that he might not find this suggestion entirely uncongenial. And see note 20.

19. This move would take some of the sting out of what I take to be an anti-Functionalist argument in David Lewis (1981). On which argument see section 6.

20. Block hinted at this view, as I have mentioned. I developed the suggestion in Lycan (1981a, pp. 47–48). It has also been picked up by Hilary Putnam (1981), Sydney Shoemaker (1981), Patricia Kitcher (1982), Terence Horgan (1984b), and Gregory Sheridan (1986) among others (Shoemaker calls it "selective parochialism").

21. The following exegesis of Lewis is not entirely faithful to his current intentions, which are more complex than I can here go into. What I shall have to say is philosophically right, I believe, but should not be construed as offering any embarrassment to Lewis himself. I am very grateful to him for extended and helpful discussion on the matter.

22. Lewis has confirmed this in correspondence.

23. Here is the point at which Lewis disagrees. His motive is rather the combination of his notion of a "typical" cause or effect, ambiguous as between typical-for-the-individual and typical-for-the-species, and his implicit-definition view of folk-theoretical terms with which I of course disagree. Notice, however, that Lewis is committed to a form of Two-Levelism, just as Shoemaker is, by way of his *analytic* functionalism; cf. note 14. Lewis does not, of course, deny the multiplicity of levels of organization that apply to the brain in fact.

24. Shoemaker (1975); see also Shoemaker (1982).

25. Block (1980). By now the reader will be firmly convinced that I hate Block and am prosecuting a vendetta against him in this book. Nothing of the sort is true; I think his "absent fluid" example and all his other anti-Functionalist speculations are ingenious and intuitively powerful, and *if one persistently thinks in Two-Level terms* one

will (otherwise) *rightly* find them almost irresistible. I merely urge everyone to give up thinking in Two-Level terms, which were never plausible to begin with.
26. What does follow from Shoemaker's 1 and 5 is

6'. $(\exists Q_?)CAUSE(Q_?(S_2),B[O_1,Q_?(S_2)]$

—which is satisfied by the "absent fluid" model.
27. As I understand him, in any case, Block is *not* willing to make the latter supposition; he wants to hold Type-Identity with respect to qualia.
28. This overlooks the fact that Shoemaker himself is an analytical functionalist, and so cannot avail himself of my way out (as he has reminded me in correspondence).

Chapter 6

1. I now rather favor the sort of theory defended by Fodor (1981), according to which my brain contains a "belief box," which is teleologically structured in such a way as to store brain items of shape so-and-so just in case such-and-such a condition obtains in the world. But the theory needs modification to remove its obvious Panglossian implications; see Lycan (forthcoming). Fodor, incidentally, seems himself to have given up the view (Fodor, 1987).
2. To say nothing of awareness of one's "self." I would not touch that issue for a free weekend at Pismo Beach. However, for a superb exposition and thorough discussion, see Rosenberg (1986).
3. In a commentary on Dennett, Michael Arbib (1972) suggested a third notion, "awareness$_{1.5}$," having to do with the concentration of attention.
4. For excellent further pursuit of a similar line, see Rosenthal (1986).
5. On attention, see Broadbent (1958, 1982), Neisser (1967), Lackner and Garrett (1973), Parasuraman and Davies (1984), and Johnston and Dark (1986).

Chapter 7

1. Actually that question—in so many words—and the concern behind it go back to Brian Farrell (1950).
2. Frank Jackson (1984) offers a significantly improved version of the argument. However, what I shall have to say against Nagel will apply to Jackson's formulation also.
3. Nagel has been widely bashed in the literature: Dennett and Hofstadter (1981), Lewis (1984), van Gulick (1985), P. M. Churchland (1985a), P. S. Churchland (1986), Tye (1986), and others. This attention is a tribute to the initial appeal of his argument; but it also seems to me that all the critics' objections are sound. (In this chapter I am only adding a few points that I have not seen made heretofore.) Pardon my mentioning it again, but if Functionalism and materialism generally are mistaken on grounds of "qualia," "subjectivity," or the like, then there must exist a sound and non-question-begging argument to show that. The point is one that seems to need repeating—not that the repetition ever seems to do any good.
4. Note too Hofstadter's remarks on pp. 406ff. about interpreting Nagel's locution and about its intended "subjectlessness." This subjectlessness is hard to pin down, since in one obvious subjectless sense there is something it is like to be *anything* doing *anything*, even a brick or a cardboard carton. ("What is it like to be a brick? Look there, at that brick—it's doing it.") For these reasons, premise 1 is obscure even before we get to 3. Norman Malcolm (in Armstrong and Malcolm, 1984) has

argued persuasively that there is simply no natural interpretation of Nagel's too celebrated phrase that supports any interesting point against materialism.

5. See Boër and Lycan (1980) for discussion of the enormous literature on this, as well as the same authors' (1986).
6. Note that the same argument works against someone who takes Castañeda's view that each of us has an irreducibly indexical *self*-concept that figures in such beliefs as my belief that *I* am in danger. Such a concept should be representable as a function from worlds to individuals. Right; *what* function? Specify it and it is not (even apparently) irreducible any more.
7. Voluminously more on this in the next chapter.
8. Note that that sense is virtually never employed in philosophical, or other, writing.
9. Lawrence Nemirow (1979) and David Lewis (1983b) suggest that whatever is distinctive about "knowing what it is like" is a matter of a skill or aptitude, a "knowing how" rather than a "knowing that." Insofar as "knowing how" is a functional condition, I would agree. But see Jackson's (forthcoming) reply to Lewis.
10. McGinn (1983) and McMullen (1985) also see and develop connections between the "subjectivity" of qualia and the "essential indexical." These connections are, I believe, well worth exploring in detail.

I thank Bob van Gulick for particularly subtle and important comments on this chapter. They are, in fact, too subtle and important for me to try to deal with before press time. But see again van Gulick (1985).

Chapter 8

1. E.g., Lewis (1929), Goodman (1951).
2. E.g., see Smart's (1959) response to "Objection 4."
3. As I have said, I believe the idea that qualia pose a terrible problem for materialism is very largely due to covert slippage into the original, first-order property conception—viz., the Banana Peel.
4. Exceptions here would be Smart (1963) and Armstrong (1979).
5. But cf. Sellars (1975) and Tye (1984).
6. A related complaint is made by Butchvarov (1980), who also draws a related conclusion.
7. E.g., by Richardson and Muilenburg (1982).
8. Cf. Sellars (1975).
9. Alternatively we could represent "homogeneously" as a predicate modifier:

$$[((\exists x)[(Homogeneously(Green))(Patch)](x))(Sensing)](Leopold).$$

This would reflect that different individuals can have the structured property of being homogeneously-green. But the difference does not affect subsequent issues.
10. Stalnaker (1968), Lewis (1973), Pollock (1976), Lycan (1984c), . . .
11. Cf. also Castañeda (1977).
12. Jackson is of course aware of this alternative, but gives it oddly short shrift, saying that its bare suggestion "is not to ex*plain* anything, it is not to put forward a *theory*. It is, rather, to draw attention to the need for one" (pp. 111–112). Of course no bare suggestion puts forward a theory; but in this case the theory has already been rather well elaborated, as I shall discuss below. (The point has also been made by Cresswell, 1980.)
13. This line of thought began in modern times with Anscombe (1965); see also Thomason (1973), Adams (1975), and Lewis (1983a).

14. For a philosophically relevant summary, see Clark (1985). And for a truly elegant discussion of color as a *quale*, see Levin (1986).

15. Toward the end of his article, Kraut himself anticipates this development. The present chapter owes a great deal to Kraut's discussion and to related personal conversations, as well as to Sellars (1975).

16. Jackson raises this point (pp. 71–72). He also insists that even if nonactual possibilia be admitted, the truth-conditions of sentences about color in particular must not include nonactual items; but he offers no argument.

17. See the papers on this topic collected in Armstrong (1981).

18. For discussion of this point I am grateful to Jack Copeland and Derek Browne.

19. In conversation. I am indebted to Gallois and to the other philosophers of the University of Queensland, as well as to Les Holborow, for a very illuminating discussion of a fledgling version of the first half of this chapter.

20. There are further, alternative implementations of Gallois' suggestion. For example, he himself recommends defining "sensing greenly" in the way recommended above, and then specifying our otherworldly object as follows: Were I to see any perceptually discriminable part of the object in the absence of the rest of the object, I would sense greenly. The choice between options here must remain the subject of another essay.

21. I believe Dennett is guilty of this in (1978a, chapter 9) and elsewhere.

22. The remaining sections of this chapter are based on a paper delivered at the Mini-Conference on Wilfrid Sellars' Philosophy of Perception, Ohio State University, May 1979; Sellars' comments on that occasion were, to say the least, disapproving. I shall remark on some of them below.

23. To avoid tedious exegesis, I must assume familiarity with Sellars' use of this term.

24. I must likewise assume acquaintance with this legendary person, who—defying the delighted horror of his Rylean contemporaries—first posited *inner episodes* having propositional and/or qualitative content that explain human behavior. (His *locus classicus* is Sellars, 1956.)

25. But see note 33.

26. See again Sellars (1975). He does not pursue the sort of semantical investigation conducted in section 2; I do not know whether he would condone it.

27. Since Sellars characterizes the Manifest Image in part by saying that the epistemic methods associated with it "[do] *not* include . . . the postulation of imperceptible entities, and principles pertaining to them, to explain the behavior of perceptible things" (1962, p. 7), it is hard to see how Jones was allowed to get away with this. I have some ideas on the point, but I shall let them pass for now.

28. See Sellars (1967, particularly chapter V); see also Hesse (1966).

29. In his comments on the paper from which the following sections of this chapter are drawn (see note 2). In further notes I shall indicate one or two of his objections to the present interpretation. I would defend my version *as* an interpretation of at least the published Sellars prior to 1980 (particularly 1962, 1965, 1971), but this is hardly the place; I shall be doing that in a separate paper. Sellars sets out what I would contend is a revisionist account of color in (1981); for a splendid and nicely irenic discussion of the exegetical issue, see Rosenberg (1982).

30. It is crucial to realize that what I am giving here is the merest outline of Argument G, with all the interesting lemmas left out. Almost all the secondary literature on the "grain" argument oversimplifies it by *anyone's* standards and so fails to see the problem of homogeneity. Two articles that (though still oversimple) seem to me to be on the right track are Delaney (1970) and Hooker (1977). There is also an excellent piece by William S. Robinson (1982). But the best I know is still Richardson

and Muilenburg (1982), which begins to go into the kind of detail required for an adequate exegesis; it has been of great help to me in trying to understand the argument. (I am also grateful to Bob Richardson, to Jay Rosenberg, and to David Rosenthal for extended conversation and correspondence on this topic.) My own attempted reconstruction of the second "grain" argument is currently running around 55 steps, but so far I have only hit the high spots. Sellars has insisted in conversation that his intended argument is not nearly so complicated; but see his (1971) for an indication of how complicated it is.

   I shall not make any attempt to evaluate the argument here, though I shall be working my way back toward it in section 9.

31. Sellars objects to this use of the morpheme "quasi-"; I am not sure why.

32. Sellars is not absolutely committed to their being particulars; I shall consider other options below.

33. In his comments on this material, Sellars insisted to the contrary that the pinkness and the cubicity of his pink ice cube are "given," and that we are "directly aware of" sensa (we must be, or we could not respond conceptually to them). What is not given, contrary to the phenomenalist tradition that Sellars has been concerned to oppose, is only the categorial status or "guise" of the pinkness and cubicity; we must philosophize at length in order to determine whether they are properties of physical objects, adverbial modes of sensing, adjectival properties of pure processes, or whatever. Moreover, the pinkness and cubicity are not subject to the analogical stretching that produces the Scientific-Image successor concept of a quasi-quasi-pink sensum; the stretching applies only to the categorial guises again. In abstraction from their guises, the pinkness and cubicity *themselves* get carried over into the Scientific Image. (According to Sellars this does not imply that objects of final microphysics are *literally* pink or cubical, since Manifest-Image categorial guise is part of the meanings of those words as we are now using them.)

34. A few traditional sense-datum accounts preserve this feature also—e.g., Jackson (1977).

35. Sellars in discussion has emphatically rejected the claim that sensa are *posited* at all, either on the microphysicists' own initiative or at the request of psychologists. Their "sensory cores," at least, are given in perception (cf. note 13). We are directly aware of them, period, even in the final Scientific Image. (Thus Sellars seems to have abandoned the third-person perspective of Jones, which was for me the main attraction of his argument as I originally understood it. Moreover, he has forfeited his claim to be a Scientific Realist in the sense of his own *scientia mensura*: "[S]cience is the measure of all things, of what it is that it is, and of what is not that it is not" (1963a, p. 173).) The neuroanatomists and the microphysicists are being asked only to *relate* their own posits to the sensa that Sellars is telling them are already there. The onus is on the scientists to show how it is that their various neurons and leptons can interact with the brown, pink, etc., sensings that are already there in the skull—needed *a priori* to be there, if the perceptual propositional attitudes are to be accounted for.

36. To put the argument a slightly different way: If we were to take a collection of molecules (assumed to have only the properties that, roughly, they are known to have at present), we could build a physical$_2$ version of a human being whose verbal behavior would be exactly like ours in appropriate circumstances. Would Sellars have to say that our simulacrum was merely an automaton? (Steven Dumpleton has pointed out to me in conversation that the simulacrum would presumably have the same Manifest-Image concepts that we do and, if he was intelligent to boot,

infer that he was partly made of sensa—and he would be wrong. I am not sure, though, that this line of reasoning does not beg the question against Sellars.)

Smart (1978) constructs an argument closely related to mine:

> . . . if it be granted that the brain is essentially a nerve net, then physics enters our understanding of the mind by way of the biochemistry and biophysics of neurons. But neurons are, in Feinberg's sense, "ordinary matter." So whatever revolutionary changes occur in physics, there will be no important lesson for the mind-body problem or for the philosophy of biology generally. . . . The situation is not like that in the eighteenth century, when physics was mainly mechanics, and needed to be supplemented by the theory of electricity and magnetism, even for the purpose of understanding the behaviour of ordinary bulk matter. (P. 340)

37. The question of shyness is somewhat though not entirely alleviated by Sellars' current denial that sensa are posited entities at all (cf. note 33).

38. Sellars objects to the thesis that a spatially extended thing necessarily has spatial parts; he thinks the parts are only "virtual."

39. Cf. again Armstrong's version of naturalism (1978 a,b). We might call Armstrong's view "physicalism$_{1.5}$." Sellars himself thinks (cf. 1981, and Smart, 1982)) that the particles of twentieth-century physics are being steadily reduced to standing waves or to pure processes, and since sensa are pure processes too, there will be no interaction problem.

40. George Pappas reminded me that Berkeley argued in something very like this way.

41. There is yet a third possibility: Even if we do give up on the idea that particles could have even quasi-quasi-color, why should we not short-circuit the first "grain" argument and posit little nonparticulate particulars *in physical objects* that have quasi-quasi-color?—*chroma*, we might call them—for that option has been available all along. Chroma are just like sensa, except that they would occur throughout space instead of hiding within sentient beings. Their occurrence within sentient beings under the right circumstances, of course, would still function as sensa do in explaining the perceptual propositional attitudes; this would reinstate a Scientific-Image version of representationalism.

There is still a problem in seeing how the microphysicist would recognize chroma when he came across them; but at least they do not suffer from shyness. And I have just suggested a way in which they might function within sentient beings to produce perceptual propositional attitudes. Unfortunately, the positing of chroma would have a nasty consequence: If chroma can double as sensa when they occur inside the central nervous systems of sentient beings, and a person who senses redly did so in virtue of hosting quasi-quasi-red chroma, it seems to follow (since chroma are what make for color in physical objects) that some part of the subject's brain is literally red—so nerves would after all be colored inside like chocolate candies.

Chapter 9

1. The moral dimension of Functionalism in particular is explored in Clifford Simak's "How-2," in T. E. Dikty (ed.), *Five Tales from Tomorrow* (New York: Fawcett Crest Books, 1957); in Stanislaw Lem's "The Seventh Sally, or How Trurl's Own Perfection Led to No Good," in *The Cyberiad*, trans. Michael Kandel (New York: Seabury Press, 1974); and by Andrew M. Greeley in *God Game* (New York: Warner Books, 1986). I

am grateful to Jan Szrednicki for recommending Lem's writings to me some years ago, and to my wife Mary for calling my attention to the Greeley novel.

2. Some fellow countryman of Sartre's has famously remarked that "tout comprendre c'est tout pardonner." *Not in the least.*

3. Admittedly there are literally irresistible urges (think of the perfect aphrodisiac, that acts directly on the muscles and glands, depriving its victim of any choice whatsoever). And what they seem to have in common is that there are *determining* causes. A person who literally could not do otherwise no matter how strongly and single-mindedly he or she wants to cannot be blamed.

4. Here I assume the correctness of Armstrong's (1973) metaphilosophical position, to the effect that as between common sense, science, and purely philosophical method (excluding formal logic), philosophy comes in a very weak third. On a combination of Peircean and Moorean grounds that I have not the space to explain here, I maintain it is impossible in principle for a purely philosophical view or "intuition" to defeat an alliance between common sense and science.

5. See also chapter VII of Levin (1979).

6. It might be rejoined that checks and money and so on have their significance conventionally, in that by common agreement we *stipulate* connections between causal chains of certain sorts and other things such as quantities of human labor that have intrinsic value. This does not seem to hold in the case of art fraud. But that case is to my mind the least secure; it *is* hard to justify our strong preference for an original over a copy, and show that that preference is not just snobbery (a classic problem in aesthetic theory).

7. However, J. L. Austin (1956) argued more forcefully against hypothetical analyses of "I could have done otherwise," on somewhat technical grounds.

8. Taylor (1974). Browsing in a bookshop, Osmo finds a complete biography of his own life, uncannily accurate up till the present and also going on to predict Osmo's death in a plane crash, which then occurs on schedule.

9. For a further, more detailed, reply to Taylor, see Goldman (1968).

10. Notably van Inwagen (1983). I take Slote (1982) to be an adequate reply to van Inwagen; however, see van Inwagen (1985).

Epilogue

1. On a number of occasions when I have delivered bits of this book as talks or lectures, one or another member of the audience has kindly praised my argumentative adroitness, dialectical skill, etc., but added that cleverness—and my arguments themselves—are quite beside the point, a mere exercise and/or display. Nagel (1979) may perhaps be read more charitably, but not much more charitably:

> I believe one should trust problems over solutions, intuition over arguments. . . . [Well, excuuuuse me!—WGL] If arguments or systematic theoretical considerations lead to results that seem intuitively not to make sense . . . , then something is wrong with the argument and more work needs to be done. Often the problem has to be reformulated, because an adequate answer to the original formulation fails to make the *sense* of the problem disappear. (Pp. x–xi)

If by this Nagel means only that intuitions contrary to ostensibly sound argument need at least to be explained away, no one would disagree (but the clause "something is wrong with the argument" discourages that interpretation). The task of explaining away "qualia"-based intuitive objections to materialism is what in large part I have undertaken in this book. If I have failed, I would like to be *shown why* (or, of course, presented with some new antimaterialist argument). To engage in further muttering and posturing would be idle.

2. Perhaps it is time for a brisk catalogue, all in one spot, of the different "qualia"-based objections we have encountered in this book, which are all the different ones I myself have encountered anywhere: (i) Early critics of the Identity Theory invoked qualia in posing Leibniz's-Law objections (see Lycan, 1972, and the references therein). (ii) Others focused on our seemingly immediate access to qualia (e.g., Baier, 1962). (iii) As was discussed in chapter 2, Saul Kripke's rejection of physicalism is based on an essentialist thesis involving qualia. (iv) Still other philosophers have pursued the sort of counterexample technique discussed in chapter 3. (v) Nagel, and Keith Gunderson (1970, 1974) before him, have worried over first-person/third-person asymmetries and the perspectival nature or point-of-view-iness of consciousness. (vi) As I have read them in chapter 7, Nagel and Frank Jackson also call our attention to what he thinks is a funny kind of *fact* that has no place in physical science. (vii) Jackson earlier argued for the existence of little colored nonphysical sense-data in (or near) the head, and we have seen in chapter 8 that the appeal to phenomenal individuals is a powerful antimaterialist force, especially when subtly introduced by way of the Banana Peel. Finally, as distinct from all these concerns, (viii) Sellars has stressed the grainlessness or *homogeneity* of sensory qualia, and maintained that that homogeneity is what prevents our dissolving qualia peacefully into a Democritean picture of the universe. If there are still more different "qualia" arguments, I have failed to discern them.

Appendix

1. The material in this appendix was first presented as part of the John Ingram Forry Lecture at Amherst College, in 1985. I am very grateful to Jay Garfield and to Lee Bowie for their penetrating formal commentaries on that occasion, which I shall be answering in the (eventually to be) published proceedings of the event.

2. Harry has appeared before, in Lycan (1985). The next four paragraphs are lifted almost *verbatim* from that article.

3. It is interesting that children seem instinctively to reject the hypothesis of machine consciousness, usually on the grounds that computers are not alive. (One day when my daughter Jane was three years old, we were fooling with some piece of software or other, and I quite unreflectively remarked "It thinks you want it to [do such-and-such]." She did an enormous take, and then replied, "Computers can't think!—Is that 'just an expression'??")

4. I borrow the term "defining technology," and the examples, from Jay Bolter (1984).

5. The computational picture of mentality is by no means new. For one thing, the idea of mechanical intelligence goes back to the seventeenth century at least, long before Charles Babbage's celebrated Analytical Engine. And the computer model of the mind received a decisive boost from the McCullough-Pitts model of the neuron (1947), according to which a neuron is nothing but a little on-off device, that either *fires* or does not. If a brain is just an organized collection of neurons, and a neuron is just an on-off switch, it follows *straightway* that a brain is a digital computer and anything interesting that it does is a computation over binary formulas. Thus a human being is not only a featherless biped, a rational animal, and the only creature on earth that laughs, but the only computing machine on earth that is made by unskilled labor.

The McCullough-Pitts model is no longer current (no pun intended): neurons are now known to be very complicated little agents, not mere on-off switches. But the computational picture of mentality still receives strong encouragement from other quarters. It has two separate philosophical motivations, in particular, the first of which I have already noted: It exploits and explains the coalescence of the notions of computation, information, and intelligence. The computer is the only thing in the world that displays potential intelligence *and* whose workings are well understood. It is the only answer we currently know to the question: By what means *could* Mother Nature have crafted an intelligent being (in our sense of responsiveness to contingencies) out of nothing but a large bunch of individually insensate biological cells? To deny that there may be other answers would be presumptuous at best, and there are plenty of human capacities that do not seem to admit of computational simulation in any way at all—but anyone who manages to think up a genuinely distinct alternative to the digital-computer paradigm will have achieved a major conceptual breakthrough. For the foreseeable future, computation is our only model for intelligence.

Computationalism as a form of Homunctionalism also affords us a way of acknowledging our place as physical organisms amid the closed causal order we call Nature, without benefit of intervention by ghosts. (Actually I hear there are some physicists who speculate that quantum indeterminacies afford gaps in nature that are in principle permeable to Cartesian minds, and that immaterial egos do insert themselves into quantum gaps, thus taking over the role of hidden variables. But (i) it would have to be shown how such quantum phenomena could be combined and multiplied into macroscopic effects characteristic of intelligence, i.e., how the brain could act as a "quantum magnifier," and (ii) to avoid *ad-hoc*ness of the crassest sort, one would have to find *physical reason* to think that Cartesian intervention does occur, which task I take to be almost definitionally impossible.)

6. Of course, this re-emphasizes the question of human freedom: if humans are just wetware or liveware, are they not then essentially soft puppets? This in turn suggests—however speciously in light of the arguments made in chapter 9—that the computational view of people must therefore be drastically wrong.

7. Relatively speaking, of course; I am not encouraging Two-Levelism.

8. That mental acts do not *feel* digital is not an objection either. To infer from that fact that mental acts are not digital would be a clear case of what Armstrong (1968a) calls the "headless woman" fallacy.

References

Adams, E. M. (1975). *Philosophy and the Modern Mind*. Chapel Hill: University of North Carolina Press.

Anscombe, G. E. M. (1965). "The Intentionality of Sensation: A Grammatical Feature." In R. J. Butler (ed.), *Analytical Philosophy: Second Series*. Oxford: Basil Blackwell.

Anscombe, G. E. M., and P. Geach, eds. (1954). *Descartes: Philosophical Writings*. London: Thomas Nelson and Sons.

Arbib, M. (1972). "Consciousness: The Secondary Role of Language." *Journal of Philosophy* 69.

Armstrong, D. M. (1961). *Perception and the Physical World*. London: Routledge and Kegan Paul.

Armstrong, D. M. (1962). *Bodily Sensations*. London: Routledge and Kegan Paul.

Armstrong, D. M. (1968a). "The Headless Woman Illusion and the Defense of Materialism." *Analysis* 29.

Armstrong, D. M. (1968b). *A Materialist Theory of the Mind*. London: Routledge and Kegan Paul.

Armstrong, D. M. (1968c). "The Secondary Qualities." *Australasian Journal of Philosophy* 46.

Armstrong, D. M. (1972). "Materialism, Properties and Predicates." *Monist* 56.

Armstrong, D. M. (1973). "Epistemological Foundations for a Materialist Theory of the Mind." *Philosophy of Science* 40. Reprinted in Armstrong (1981).

Armstrong, D. M. (1978a). "Naturalism, Materialism, and First Philosophy," *Philosophia* 8. Reprinted in Armstrong (1981).

Armstrong, D. M. (1978b). *Universals and Scientific Realism* (in two volumes). Cambridge: Cambridge University Press.

Armstrong, D. M. (1979). "Perception, Sense Data and Causality." In G. F. Macdonald (ed.), *Perception and Identity: Essays Presented to A. J. Ayer with His Replies to Them*. London: Macmillan. Reprinted in Armstrong (1981).

Armstrong, D. M. (1981). The Nature of Mind *and Other Essays*. Ithaca: Cornell University Press.

Armstrong, D. M., and N. Malcolm (1984). *Consciousness and Causality*. Oxford: Basil Blackwell.

Attneave, F. (1960). "In Defense of Homunculi." In W. Rosenblith (ed.), *Sensory Communication*. Cambridge, MA: MIT Press.

Austin, J. L. (1956). "If and Cans." *Proceedings of the British Academy* 42. Reprinted in *Philosophical Papers*. Oxford: Oxford University Press, 1961.

Ayer, A. J. (1954). "Freedom and Necessity." In *Philosophical Essays*. London: Macmillan.

Baier, K. (1962). "Smart on Sensations." *Australasian Journal of Philosophy* 40.

Bechtel, P. W. (1983). "A Bridge between Cognitive Science and Neuroscience: The Functional Architecture of Mind." *Philosophical Studies* 44.

Bechtel, P. W. (1985). "Contemporary Connectionism: Are the New Parallel Distributed Processing Models Cognitive or Associationist?" *Behaviorism* 13.

Bennett, J. (1976). *Linguistic Behavior*. Cambridge: Cambridge University Press.

Bigelow, J., and R. Pargetter (1986). "Functions." Presented to the Australasian Association of Philosophy, Melbourne.

Biro, J. (1981). "Persons as Corporate Entities and Corporations as Persons." *Nature and System* 3.

Block, N. J. (1978). "Troubles with Functionalism." In W. Savage (ed.), *Perception and Cognition: Minnesota Studies in the Philosophy of Science, Vol. IX.* Minneapolis: University of Minnesota Press.

Block, N. J. (1980). "Are Absent Qualia Impossible?" *Philosophical Review* 89.

Block, N. J. (1981a). "Psychologism and Behaviorism." *Philosophical Review* 90.

Block, N. J., ed. (1981b). *Readings in Philosophy of Psychology, Vol. I.* Cambridge, MA: Harvard University Press.

Boër, S., and W. G. Lycan (1980). "Who, Me?" *Philosophical Review* 89.

Boër, S., and W. G. Lycan (1986). *Knowing Who.* Cambridge, MA: MIT Press/Bradford Books.

Bolter, J. (1984). *Turing's Man.* Chapel Hill: University of North Carolina Press.

Bradley, M. C. (1964). "Critical Notice of J. J. C. Smart's *Philosophy and Scientific Realism.*" *Australasian Journal of Philosophy* 42.

Bradley, M. C. (1963). "Sensations, Brain-Processes, and Colours." *Australasian Journal of Philosophy* 41.

Broadbent, D. E. (1958). *Perception and Communication.* Oxford: Pergamon Press.

Broadbent, D. E. (1982). "Task Combination and Selective Intake of Information." *Acta Psychologica* 50.

Brooks, D. H. M. (1986). "Group Minds." *Australasian Journal of Philosophy* 64.

Burge, T. (1979). "Individualism and the Mental." In P. French, T. E. Uehling, and H. Wettstein (eds.), *Midwest Studies in Philosophy, Vol. IV: Studies in Metaphysics.* Minneapolis: University of Minnesota Press.

Bush, E. (1974). "Rorty Revisited." *Philosophical Studies* 25.

Butchvarov, P. (1980). "Adverbial Theories of Consciousness." In P. French, T. E. Uehling, and H. Wettstein (eds.), *Midwest Studies in Philosophy, Vol. V: Studies in Epistemology.* Minneapolis: University of Minnesota Press.

Campbell, C. A. (1957). *On Selfhood and Godhood.* London: Allen and Unwin.

Campbell, K. K. (1969). "Colours." In R. Brown and C. D. Rollins (eds.), *Contemporary Philosophy in Australia.* London: Allen and Unwin.

Campbell, K. K. (1970). *Body and Mind.* New York: Doubleday Anchor Books.

Carnap, R. (1932/33). "Psychology in Physical Language." *Erkenntnis* 3.

Castañeda, H.-N. (1966). "He*: A Study in the Logic of Self-Consciousness." *Ratio* 8.

Castañeda, H.-N. (1977). "Perception, Belief, and the Structure of Physical Objects and Consciousness." *Synthese* 35.

Chappell, V. C. (ed.) (1962). *The Philosophy of Mind.* Englewood Cliffs, NJ: Prentice-Hall.

Chisholm, R. (1946). "The Contrary-to-Fact Conditional." *Mind* 55.

Chisholm, R. (1957). *Perceiving.* Ithaca: Cornell University Press.

Churchland, P. M. (1984). *Matter and Consciousness.* Cambridge, MA: MIT Press/Bradford Books.

Churchland, P., M. (1985a). "Reduction, Qualia, and the Direct Introspection of Brain States." *Journal of Philosophy* 82.

Churchland, P. M. (1985b). "On Representation, Computation, and Implementation: A New Theory of How the Brain Works." Typescript, University of California at San Diego.

Churchland, P. M. (1986). "Some Reductive Strategies in Cognitive Neurobiology." *Mind* 95.

Churchland, P. M., and P. S. Churchland (1981). "Functionalism, Qualia, and Intentionality." *Philosophical Topics* 12.

Churchland, P. S. (1983). "Consciousness: The Transmutation of a Concept." *Pacific Philosophical Quarterly* 64.

Churchland, P. S. (1986). *Neurophilosophy.* Cambridge, MA: MIT Press/Bradford Books.

Clark, A. (1985). "Qualia and the Psychophysiological Explanation of Color Perception." *Synthese* 65.

Clark, R. (1970). "Concerning the Logic of Predicate Modifiers." *Nous* 4.

Cornman, J. (1974). "Can Eddington's 'Two' Tables Be Identical?" *Australasian Journal of Philosophy* 52.

Cresswell, M. J. (1980). "Jackson on Perception." *Theoria* 46.

Cummins, R. (1983). *The Nature of Psychological Explanation*. Cambridge, MA: MIT Press/ Bradford Books.

Davidson, D. (1970). "Mental Events." In Foster and Swanson (eds.), *Experience and Theory*. Amherst: University of Massachusetts Press.

Davis, L. (1974). "Functional Definitions and How It Feels to Be in Pain." Mimeo, University of Missouri, St. Louis.

Davis, L. (1982). "Functionalism and Absent Qualia." *Philosophical Studies* 41.

Delaney, C. F. (1970). "Sellars' Grain Argument." *Australasian Journal of Philosophy* 50.

Dennett, D. C. (1969). *Content and Consciousness*. London: Routledge and Kegan Paul.

Dennett, D. C. (1975). "Why the Law of Effect Will Not Go Away." *Journal of the Theory of Social Behavior* 5. Reprinted in Dennett (1978a).

Dennett, D. C. (1978a). *Brainstorms*. Montgomery, VT: Bradford Books.

Dennett, D. C. (1978b). "Skinner Skinned." In Dennett (1978a).

Dennett, D. C. (1978c). "Why You Can't Make a Computer That Feels Pain." *Synthese* 38. Reprinted in Dennett (1978a).

Dennett, D. C. (1979). "On the Absence of Phenomenology." In B. L. Tapscott and D. Gustafson (eds.), *Body, Mind and Method: Essays in Honor of Virgil Aldrich*. Dordrecht: D. Reidel.

Dennett, D. C. (1982). "How to Study Consciousness Empirically: Or, Nothing Comes to Mind." *Synthese* 53.

Dennett, D. C. (forthcoming-a). "The Logical Geography of Computational Approaches (a View from the East Pole)." In M. Brand and R. M. Harnish (eds.), *The Representation of Knowledge and Belief*. Tucson: University of Arizona Press.

Dennett, D. C. (forthcoming-b). "Quining Qualia." In a volume ed. by A. Marcel and E. Bisiach, Como, Italy. To be reprinted in Dennett's forthcoming *The Intentional Stance* (Cambridge MA: MIT Press/Bradford Books).

Dennett, D. C., and D. Hofstadter (1981). *The Mind's I*. New York: Basic Books.

Dretske, F. (1981). *Knowledge and the Flow of Information*. Cambridge, MA: MIT Press/ Bradford Books.

Dreyfus, H. (1979). *What Computers Can't Do* (rev. ed.). New York: Harper Colophon Books.

Eddington, A. (1935). *The Nature of the Physical World*. London: J. M. Dent and Sons, Ltd.

Elugardo, R. (1981). "Machine Functionalism and the New Lilliputian Argument." *Pacific Philosophical Quarterly* 62.

Elugardo, R. (1983). "Machine Realization and the New Lilliputian Argument." *Philosophical Studies* 43.

Farrell, B. A. (1950). "Experience." *Mind* 59.

Feldman, F. (1974). "Kripke on the Identity Theory." *Journal of Philosophy* 71.

Feldman, F. (1981). "Identity, Necessity, and Events." In Block (1981b).

Field, H. (1978). "Mental Representation." *Erkenntnis* 13.

Fodor, J. A. (1968a). "The Appeal to Tacit Knowledge in Psychological Explanation." *Journal of Philosophy* 65.

Fodor, J. A. (1968b). *Psychological Explanation*. New York: Random House.

Fodor, J. A. (1975). *The Language of Thought*. New York: Thomas Y. Crowell.

Fodor, J. A. (1978). "Propositional Attitudes." *Monist* 61. Reprinted in Fodor (1981).

Fodor, J. A. (1981). *RePresentations*. Cambridge, MA: MIT Press/Bradford Books.

Fodor, J. A. (1984). "Semantics, Wisconsin Style." *Synthese* 59.

Fodor, J. A. (1981). "Psychosemantics, or: Where Do Truth-Conditions Come From?" Typescript, MIT.

Fodor, J. A. (1987). *Psychosemantics*. In preparation.

Fodor, J. A., and N. J. Block (1972a). "What Psychological States Are Not." *Philosophical Review* 81.

Fodor, J. A., and N. J. Block (1972b). "Cognitivism and the Analog/Digital Distinction." Unpublished typescript, MIT.

French, P. (1984). *Collective and Corporate Responsibility.* New York: Columbia University Press.

Geach, P. (1957). *Mental Acts.* London: Routledge and Kegan Paul.

Goldman, A. I. (1968). "Actions, Predictions, and Books of Life." *American Philosophical Quarterly* 5.

Goodman, N. (1947). "The Problem of Counterfactual Conditionals." *Journal of Philosophy* 44.

Goodman, N. (1951). *The Structure of Appearance.* Indianapolis: Bobbs-Merrill.

Gunderson, K. (1970). "Asymmetries and Mind-Body Perplexities." In M. Radner and S. Winokur (eds.), *Minnesota Studies in the Philosophy of Science,* Vol. IV. Minneapolis: University of Minnesota Press.

Gunderson, K. (1974). "The Texture of Mentality." In R. Bambrough (ed.), *Wisdom— Twelve Essays.* Oxford: Oxford University Press.

Gunderson, K. (1985). *Mentality and Machines* (2nd ed.). Minneapolis: University of Minnesota Press.

Hardin, C. L. (1985). "Qualia and Materialism: Closing the Explanatory Gap." Presented at the American Philosophical Association (Eastern Division) Meetings, 1985; abstracted in *Journal of Philosophy* 82.

Harrison, B. (1973). *Form and Content.* Oxford: Basil Blackwell.

Haugeland, J. (1978). "The Nature and Plausibility of Cognitivism." *Behavioral and Brain Sciences* 2.

Haugeland, J. (1981). "Analog and Analog." *Philosophical Topics* 12.

Heisenberg, W. (1937). "Gedanken der antiken Naturphilosophie in der modernen Physik." *Die Antike.*

Hesse, M. (1966). *Models and Analogies in Science.* Notre Dame: University of Notre Dame Press.

Hill, C. S. (1981). "Why Cartesian Intuitions Are Compatible with the Identity Thesis." *Philosophy and Phenomenological Research* 42.

Hill, C. S. (1986). "Introspective Awareness of Sensations." Typescript, University of Arkansas.

Hintikka, K. J. J. (1969). "On the Logic of Perception." In *Models for Modalities.* D. Reidel: Dordrecht.

Hofstadter, D. (1981). "Reflections" (on Nagel, 1974). In Dennett and Hofstadter (1981).

Hooker, C. A. (1977). "Sellars on the Inevitability of the Secondary Qualities." *Philosophical Studies* 32.

Horgan, T. (1984a). "Functionalism and Token Physicalism." *Synthese* 59.

Horgan, T. (1984b). "Functionalism, Qualia, and the Inverted Spectrum." *Philosophy and Phenomenological Research* 44.

Horgan, T. (1984c). "Jackson on Physical Information and Qualia." *Philosophical Quarterly* 34.

Hospers, J. (1958). "What Means This Freedom?" In S. Hook (ed.), *Determinism and Freedom in the Age of Modern Science.* New York: New York University Press.

Hume, D. (1739). *A Treatise of Human Nature.* London. Modern edition by L. A. Selby-Bigge (Oxford: Clarendon Press, 1946).

Hume, D. (1748). *Enquiry Concerning Human Understanding.* London. Modern edition by Charles W. Hendel (Indianapolis: Bobbs-Merrill, 1955).

Jackson, F. (1977). *Perception.* Cambridge: Cambridge University Press.

Jackson, F. (1982). "Epiphenomenal Qualia." *Philosophical Quarterly* 32.

Jackson, F. (1986). "What Mary Didn't Know." *Journal of Philosophy* 83.

Jackson, F., R. Pargetter, and E. Prior (1982). "Functionalism and Type-Type Identity Theories." *Philosophical Studies* 42.

Jacoby, H. (1985). "Eliminativism, Meaning, and Qualitative States." *Philosophical Studies* 47.

Johnston, W. A., and V. J. Dark (1986). "Selective Attention." *Annual Review of Psychology* 37.

Kim, J. (1966). "On the Psycho-Physical Identity Theory." *American Philosophical Quarterly* 3.

Kirk, R. (1974a). "Sentience and Behaviour." *Mind* 83.

Kirk, R. (1974b). "Zombies *v.* Materialists." *Aristotelian Society Supplementary Volume* 48.

Kitcher, P. S. (1982). "Two Versions of the Identity Theory." *Erkenntnis* 17.

Kraut, R. (1982). "Sensory States and Sensory Objects." *Nous* 16.

Kripke, S. (1971). "Identity and Necessity." In M. Munitz (ed.), *Identity and Individuation*. New York: New York University Press.

Kripke, S. (1972). "Naming and Necessity." In D. Davidson and G. Harman (eds.), *Semantics of Natural Language*. Dordrecht: D. Reidel.

Kripke, S. (1982). *Wittgenstein on Rules and Private Language*. Cambridge, MA: Harvard University Press.

Lackner, J. R., and M. Garrett (1973). "Resolving Ambiguity: Effects of Biasing Context in the Unattended Ear." *Cognition* 1.

Leplin, J. (1979). "Theoretical Explanation and the Mind-Body Problem" *Philosophia* 8.

Levin, J. (1985). "Functionalism and the Argument from Conceivability." *Canadian Journal of Philosophy Supplementary Volume* 11.

Levin, J. (1986). "Could Love Be Like a Heatwave?: Physicalism and the Subjective Character of Experience." *Philosophical Studies* 49.

Levin, M. (1979). *Metaphysics and the Mind-Body Problem*. Oxford: Oxford University Press.

Levine, J. (1983). "Materialism and Qualia: The Explanatory Gap." *Pacific Philosophical Quarterly* 64.

Lewis, C. I. (1929). *Mind and the World Order*. New York: C. Scribner's Sons.

Lewis, D. (1966). "An Argument for the Identity Theory." *Journal of Philosophy* 63.

Lewis, D. (1971). "Analog and Digital." *Nous* 5.

Lewis, D. (1972). "Psychophysical and Theoretical Identifications." *Australasian Journal of Philosophy* 50.

Lewis, D. (1973). *Counterfactuals*. Cambridge, MA: Harvard University Press.

Lewis, D. (1981). "Mad Pain and Martian Pain." In Block (1981b).

Lewis, D. (1983a). "Individuation by Acquaintance and by Stipulation." *Philosophical Review* 92.

Lewis, D. (1983b). "Knowing What It's Like." Postscript to "Mad Pain and Martian Pain," as reprinted in *Philosophical Papers, Vol. 1*. Oxford: Oxford University Press.

Lycan, W. G. (1971). "Recent Work on Wittgenstein's 'Criteria.'" *American Philosophical Quarterly* 8.

Lycan, W. G. (1972). "Materialism and Leibniz' Law." *Monist* 56.

Lycan, W. G. (1973). "Inverted Spectrum." *Ratio* 15.

Lycan, W. G. (1974a). "Kripke and the Materialists." *Journal of Philosophy* 71.

Lycan, W. G. (1974b). "Mental States and Putnam's Functionalist Hypothesis." *Australasian Journal of Philosophy* 52.

Lycan, W. G. (1979a). "A New Lilliputian Argument against Machine Functionalism." *Philosophical Studies* 35.

Lycan, W. G. (1979b). "The Trouble with Possible Worlds." In M. Loux (ed.), *The Possible and the Actual*. Ithaca: Cornell University Press.

Lycan, W. G. (1981a). "Form, Function, and Feel." *Journal of Philosophy* 78.

Lycan, W. G. (1981b). "Psychological Laws." *Philosophical Topics* 12.

Lycan, W. G. (1981c). "Toward a Homuncular Theory of Believing." *Cognition and Brain Theory* 4.

Lycan, W. G. (1982). "Notes on the 'KK' Thesis." Memo, University of North Carolina.

Lycan, W. G. (1983). "The Moral of the New Lilliputian Argument." *Philosophical Studies* 43.

Lycan, W. G. (1984a). *Logical Form in Natural Language*. Cambridge, MA: MIT Press/Bradford Books.

Lycan, W. G. (1984b). "Skinner and the Mind-Body Problem." *Behavioral and Brain Sciences* 7.

Lycan, W. G. (1984c). "A Syntactically Motivated Theory of Conditionals." In P. French, T. E. Uehling, and H. Wettstein (eds.), *Midwest Studies in Philosophy, Vol. IX: Causation and Causal Theories.* Minneapolis: University of Minnesota Press.

Lycan, W. G. (1985). "The Paradox of Naming." In B.-K. Matilal and J. Shaw (eds.), *Analytical Philosophy in Comparative Perspective.* Dordrecht: D. Reidel.

Lycan, W. G. (1986). "Abortion and the Civil Rights of Machines." In N. Potter and M. Timmons (eds.), *Morality and Universality.* Dordrecht: D. Reidel.

Lycan, W. G. (1987). "Phenomenal Objects: A Backhanded Defense." In J. Tomberlin (ed.), *Philosophical Perspectives,* Vol. 1.

Lycan, W. G. (forthcoming). "Ideas of Representation." In a Festschrift for E. M. Adams, ed. by David Weissbord. Totowa, NJ: Rowman and Allanheld.

Lycan, W. G., and S. Shapiro (1987). "Actuality and Essence." In P. French, T. E. Uehling, and H. Wettstein (eds.), *Midwest Studies in Philosophy, Vol. XI.* Minneapolis: University of Minnesota Press.

MacKenzie, A. W. (1972). "An Analysis of Purposive Behavior." Cornell University doctoral dissertation.

Matthen, M., and E. Levy (1984). "Teleology, Error, and the Human Immune System." *Journal of Philosophy* 81.

McCullough, W. S., and W. Pitts (1943). "A Logical Calculus of the Ideas Immanent in Nervous Activity." *Bulletin of Mathematical Biophysics* 5.

McCullough, W. S., and W. Pitts (1947). "How We Know Universals." *Bulletin of Mathematical Biophysics* 9.

McGinn, C. (1981). "Anomalous Monism and Kripke's Cartesian Intuitions." In Block (1981b).

McGinn, C. (1983). *The Subjective View.* Oxford: Oxford University Press.

McInerney, P. (1979). "Self-Determination and the Project." *Journal of Philosophy* 76.

McMullen, C. (1984). "An Argument against the Identity Theory." *Pacific Philosophical Quarterly* 65.

McMullen, C. (1985). " 'Knowing What It's Like' and the Essential Indexical." *Philosophical Studies* 48.

Mellick, D. (1973). "Behavioral Strata." Ohio State University doctoral dissertation.

Melzack, R. (1973). *The Puzzle of Pain.* Harmondsworth: Penguin Books.

Melzack, R., and P. D. Wall (1970). "Psychophysiology of Pain." In H. Yamamura (ed.), *Anesthesia and Neurophysiology, International Anesthesiology Clinics* 8.

Millikan, R. G. (1984). *Language, Thought, and Other Biological Categories.* Cambridge, MA: MIT Press/Bradford Books.

Nagel, T. (1974). "What Is It Like to Be a Bat?" *Philosophical Review* 82.

Nagel, T. (1979). "Preface" to *Mortal Questions.* Cambridge: Cambridge University Press.

Neander, K. (1981). "Teleology in Biology." Typescript, University of Adelaide.

Neander, K. (1983). "Abnormal Psychobiology." La Trobe University doctoral dissertation.

Neisser, U. (1967). *Cognitive Psychology.* New York: Appleton Century Crofts.

Nemirow, L. (1979). "Functionalism and the Subjective Quality of Experience." Stanford University doctoral dissertation.

Nemirow, L. (1980). "Review of Nagel's *Mortal Questions.*" *Philosophical Review* 89.

Noren, S. (1975). "Cornman on the Colour of Micro-Entities." *Australasian Journal of Philosophy* 53.

Parasuraman, R., and D. R. Davies, eds. (1984). *Varieties of Attention.* New York: Academic Press.

Pellionisz, A., and R. Llinas (1979). "Brain Modelling by Tensor Network Theory and Computer Simulation. The Cerebellum: Distributed Processor for Predictive Coordination." *Neuroscience* 4.

Pellionisz, A., and R. Llinas (1982). "Space-Time Representation in the Brain. The Cerebellum as a Predictive Space-Time Metric Tensor." *Neuroscience* 7.

Pitcher, G. (1971). *A Theory of Perception.* Princeton: Princeton University Press.

Place, U. T. (1956). "Is Consciousness a Brain Process?" *British Journal of Psychology* 47. Reprinted in Chappell (1962).

Pollock, J. (1976). *Subjunctive Reasoning*. Dordrecht: D. Reidel.

Poppel, E., R. Held, and D. Frost (1973). "Residual Function after Brain Wounds Involving the Central Visual Pathways in Man." *Nature* 243.

Popper, K. (1972). "Of Clouds and Clocks: An Approach to the Problem of Rationality and the Freedom of Man." In *Objective Knowledge: An Evolutionary Approach*. Oxford: Oxford University Press.

Putnam, H. (1960). "Minds and Machines." In S. Hook (ed.), *Dimensions of Mind*. New York: New York University Press.

Putnam, H. (1967). "Psychological Predicates." In W. H. Capitan and D. D. Merrill (eds.), *Art, Mind, and Religion*. Pittsburgh: University of Pittsburgh Press.

Putnam, H. (1969). "On Properties." In N. Rescher (ed.), *Essays in Honor of Carl G. Hempel*. Dordrecht: D. Reidel.

Putnam, H. (1975). "The Meaning of 'Meaning'." In K. Gunderson (ed.), *Minnesota Studies in the Philosophy of Science, Vol. VII: Language, Mind and Knowledge*. Minneapolis: University of Minnesota Press.

Putnam, H. (1981). *Reason, Truth, and History*. Cambridge: Cambridge University Press.

Rey, G. (1986). "A Puzzle about Consciousness." Typescript, University of Colorado.

Richardson, R. C. (1983). "Computational Models of Mind." Unpublished monograph, University of Cincinnati.

Richardson, R. C., and G. Muilenburg (1982). "Sellars and Sense Impressions." *Erkenntnis* 17.

Roberts, L. (1985). "Problems about Material and Formal Modes in the Necessity of Identity." *Journal of Philosophy* 82.

Robinson, W. S. (1982). "Sellarsian Materialism." *Philosophy of Science* 49.

Rorty, R. (1965). "Mind-Body Identity, Privacy, and Categories." *Review of Metaphysics* 19.

Rosenberg, J. F. (1982). "The Place of Color in the Scheme of Things: A Roadmap to Sellars' Carus Lectures." *Monist* 65.

Rosenberg, J. F. (1986). *The Thinking Self*. Philadelphia: Temple University Press.

Rosenthal, D. (1976). "Mentality and Neutrality." *Journal of Philosophy* 73.

Rosenthal, D. (1983). "Reductionism and Knowledge." In L. S. Cauman et al. (eds.), *How Many Questions?* Indianapolis: Hackett Publishing.

Rosenthal, D. (1986). "Two Concepts of Consciousness." *Philosophical Studies* 49.

Ryle, G. (1949). *The Concept of Mind*. New York: Barnes and Noble.

Sartre, J.-P. (1946). *L'Existentialism est une Humanisme*. Paris: Editions Nagel.

Sartre, J.-P. (1956). *Being and Nothingness*. Trans. Hazel E. Barnes. New York: Philosophical Library.

Searle, J. (1980). "Minds, Brains and Programs." *Behavioral and Brain Sciences* 3.

Sellars, W. S. (1956). "Empiricism and the Philosophy of Mind." In H. Feigl and M. Scriven (eds.), *Minnesota Studies in the Philosophy of Science*, Vol. I. Minneapolis: University of Minnesota Press. Reprinted in Sellars (1963a).

Sellars, W. S. (1960). "Being and Being Known." *Proceedings of the American Catholic Philosophical Association* 35. Reprinted in Sellars (1963a).

Sellars, W. S. (1962). "Philosophy and the Scientific Image of Man." In R. Colodny (ed.), *Frontiers of Science and Philosophy*. Pittsburgh: University of Pittsburgh Press. Reprinted in Sellars (1963a).

Sellars, W. S. (1963a). *Science, Perception, and Reality*. London: Routledge and Kegan Paul.

Sellars, W. S. (1963b). "Phenomenalism." In Sellars (1963a).

Sellars, W. S. (1965). "The Identity Approach to the Mind-Body Problem" *Review of Metaphysics* 18.

Sellars, W. S. (1967). *Science and Metaphysics*. London: Routledge and Kegan Paul.

Sellars, W. S. (1969). "Language as Thought and as Communication." *Philosophy and Phenomenological Research* 29.

Sellars, W. S. (1971). "Seeing, Sense Impressions, and Sensa: A Reply to Cornman." *Review of Metaphysics* 24.

Sellars, W. S. (1973). "Reply to Quine." *Synthese* 26.

Sellars, W. S. (1975). "The Adverbial Theory of the Objects of Sensation," *Metaphilosophy* 6.

Sellars, W. S. (1978). "Some Reflections on Perceptual Consciousness." Typescript, University of Pittsburgh.

Sellars, W. S. (1981). "Foundations for a Metaphysics of Pure Process" (the Carus Lectures for 1977–78). *Monist* 64.

Sellars, W. S., and P. Meehl (1958). "The Concept of Emergence." In H. Feigl and M. Scriven (eds.), *Minnesota Studies in the Philosophy of Science*, Vol. I. Minneapolis: University of Minnesota Press.

Sher, G. (1977). "Kripke, Cartesian Intuitions, and Materialism." *Canadian Journal of Philosophy* 7.

Sheridan, G. (1983). "Can There Be Moral Subjects in a Physicalistic Universe?" *Philosophy and Phenomenological Research* 43.

Sheridan, G. (1986). "Selective Parochialism and Shoemaker's Argument for Functionalism." Typescript, Western Michigan University.

Shoemaker, S. (1975). "Functionalism and Qualia." *Philosophical Studies* 27.

Shoemaker, S. (1981). "Some Varieties of Functionalism." *Philosophical Topics* 12.

Shoemaker, S. (1982). "The Inverted Spectrum." *Journal of Philosophy* 79.

Simon, H. (1969). "The Architecture of Complexity." In his Compton Lectures, *The Sciences of the Artificial*. Cambridge, MA: MIT Press.

Skinner, B. F. (1984). "Representations and Misrepresentations." ("Author's Response" to Open Peer commentary on a reprinting of his article "Behaviorium at Fifty.") *Behavioral and Brain Sciences* 7.

Slote, M. A. (1982). "Selective Necessity and the Free-Will Problem." *Journal of Philosophy* 79.

Smart, J. J. C. (1959). "Sensations and Brain Processes." *Philosophical Review* 68. Reprinted in Chappell (1962).

Smart, J. J. C. (1963). *Philosophy and Scientific Realism*. London: Routledge and Kegan Paul.

Smart, J. J. C. (1978). "The Content of Physicalism." *Philosophical Quarterly* 28.

Smart, J. J. C. (1982). "Sellars on Process." *Monist* 65.

Sober, E. (1985). "Panglossian Functionalism and the Philosophy of Mind." *Synthese* 64.

Stace, W. T. (1952). *Religion and the Modern Mind*. New York: Lippincott/Harper and Row.

Stalnaker, R. (1968). "A Theory of Conditionals." *American Philosophical Quarterly Monograph*, No. 2.

Stich, S. P. (1978). "Autonomous Psychology and the Belief-Desire Thesis." *Monist* 61.

Stich, S. P. (1981). "Dennett on Intentional Systems." *Philosophical Topics* 12.

Taylor, R. (1974). *Metaphysics* (2nd ed.). Englewood Cliffs, NJ: Prentice-Hall.

Thomas, L. (1974). *Lives of a Cell*. New York: Bantam Books.

Thomason, R. (1973). "Perception and Individuation." In M. Munitz (ed.), *Logic and Ontology*. New York: New York University Press.

Tye, M. (1983). "Functionalism and Type Physicalism." *Philosophical Studies* 44.

Tye, M. (1984). "The Adverbial Approach to Visual Experience." *Philosophical Review* 93.

Tye, M. (1986). "The Subjectivity of Experience." *Mind* 95.

van Gulick, R. (1980). "Functionalism, Information, and Content." *Nature and System* 2.

van Gulick, R. (1982). "Mental Representation—a Functionalist View." *Pacific Philosophical Quarterly* 63.

van Gulick, R. (1985). "Physicalism and the Subjectivity of the Mental." *Philosophical Topics* 16.

van Inwagen, P. (1983). *An Essay on Free Will*. Oxford: Oxford University Press.

van Inwagen, P. (1985). "Modal Inference and the Free-Will Problem." Typescript, Syracuse University.

Weiskrantz, L., et al. (1974). "Visual Capacity in the Hemianopic Field Following a Restricted Occipital Ablation." *Brain* 97.

White, S. (1985). "Curse of the Qualia." Typescript, New York University.

Wimsatt, W. C. (1972). "Teleology and the Logical Structure of Function Statements." *Studies in the History and Philosophy of Science* 3.

Wimsatt, W. C. (1976). "Reductionism, Levels of Organization, and the Mind-Body Problem" In G. Globus, G. Maxwell, and I. Savodnik (eds.), *Consciousness and the Brain*. New York: Plenum.

Wright, L. (1973). "Functions." *Philosophical Review* 82.

Ziff, P. (1957/58). "About Behaviorism." *Analysis* 18. Reprinted in Chappell (1962).

Index